MASTER YOUR EMOTIONS

A Practical Guide to Overcome Negativity through Emotional Intelligence, Manage Your Feelings with Anger Management Techniques and Declutter Your Deceptive Tricky Mind

By: David Drive

**Copyright © 2019 – David Drive
All rights reserved**

The content contained within this book may not be reproduced, duplicated or transmitted without direct written permission from the author or the publisher.

Under no circumstances will any blame or legal responsibility be held against the publisher, or author, for any damages, reparation, or monetary loss due to the information contained within this book. Either directly or indirectly.

Legal Notice:
This book is copyright protected. This book is only for personal use. You cannot amend, distribute, sell, use, quote or paraphrase any part, or the content within this book, without the consent of the author or publisher.

Disclaimer Notice:
Please note the information contained within this document is for educational and entertainment purposes only. All effort has been executed to present accurate, up to date, and reliable, complete information. No warranties of any kind are declared or implied. Readers acknowledge that the author is not engaging in the rendering of legal, financial, medical or professional advice. The content within this book has been derived from various sources. Please consult a licensed professional before attempting any techniques outlined in this book.

By reading this document, the reader agrees that under no circumstances is the author responsible for any losses, direct or indirect, which are incurred as a result of the use of information contained within this document, including, but not limited to errors, omissions, or inaccuracies.

Table of Contents

Introduction 1
Chapter 1: What Emotions Are and How They Work ... 3
Chapter 2: How to Control and Change Emotions through Emotional Intelligence Concepts 33
    A Comprehensive Definition of Emotional Intelligence ... 33
    Attributes that defines Emotional Intelligence 34
    Benefits of Teaching Emotional Intelligence in Schools .. 35
    Importance of Emotional Intelligence 37
    How to Control and Change Emotions through Emotional Intelligence Concepts 55
    Advantages of Managing Emotions Using Emotional Intelligence Concepts 64
Chapter 3: Strategies to Eliminate Negative Thoughts, Stress, and Fears 68
    Strategies to Overcome Negative Thoughts 69
        Always strive to find the positive side of the situation 69
        Do not listen to people's opinions 70
        Stop thinking about the thought............................ 70
        Talk to someone.. 71
        List down the negative thoughts........................... 72
        Avoid using negative terms 73
        Talk to yourself about the thought........................ 73
        Understand and accept that you are thinking negatively 74
    Strategies to Eliminate Stress 76
        Identify the root of the stress 76
        Get rid of commitments that are not necessary......... 77
        Avoid postponing 77
        Be organized.. 78
        Do not be late 79
        Do not control others or things 80
        Avoid people who stress you out 81

    Appreciate everything and everyone in life................81
    Exercise and eat foods that are healthy....................82
    Plan to do important things only 83
    Do what you like most...83
    Talk to someone..84
    Be assertive 85
    Take caffeine in regular amounts 85
  Strategies to Eliminate Our Fears 87
    Know what your fears are 87
    Learn to appreciate...87
    Discover what emotions are associated with fear 88
    List them down 89
    Talk to someone..90
    Learn not to control things 90
    Learn from others...91
    Pray or meditate 92
    Accept that everyone makes mistakes 93
    Let life be..93
Chapter 4: Strategies of Anger Management to Reach Calmness and Build-Up Self Control 97
Chapter 5: How to Use Your Emotions for Personal Growth and to Improve Relationships 127
  Become Aware of Yourself.. 129
  Practice Self-Management... 132
  Improve Your Conflict Resolution Skills..................... 136
    Understand the conflict.. 137
    Understand the Needs of The Other Person............. 138
    Be Willing to Compromise 139
    Focus on the Conflict In Front of You 140
    Be Willing to Let Go 141
    Pick Your Battles 141
Conclusion... 160

Introduction

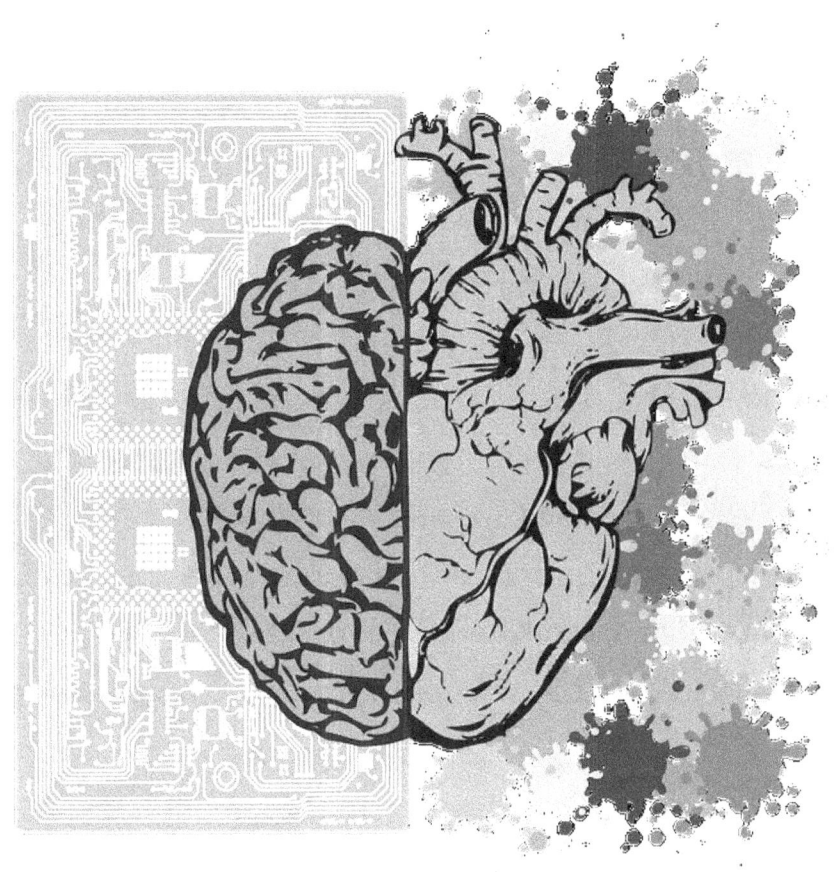

Congratulations on choosing *Master Your Emotions: A Practical Guide to Overcome Negativity through Emotional Intelligence, Manage Your Feelings with Anger Management Techniques and Declutter Your Deceptive Tricky Mind*, and thank you for doing so.

This book is a step-by-step guide for a more fulfilling life which demonstrates clearly how to identify and redirect harmful thoughts.

It teaches specific tactics to use when emotions get out of control trough a lot of examples to illustrate how the techniques described work.

Among others, this book contains the following topics:
- What emotions are and how work
- How to control and change emotions through emotional intelligence concepts
- Strategies to eliminate negative thoughts, stress and fears
- Strategies of anger management to reach calmness and build up self-control
- How to use your emotions for personal growth and to improve relationships

There are many other books about emotions management, but you chose this one. Thanks again. Every effort was put into the writing of this book to make it as useful as possible. Please enjoy!

Chapter 1: What Emotions Are and How They Work

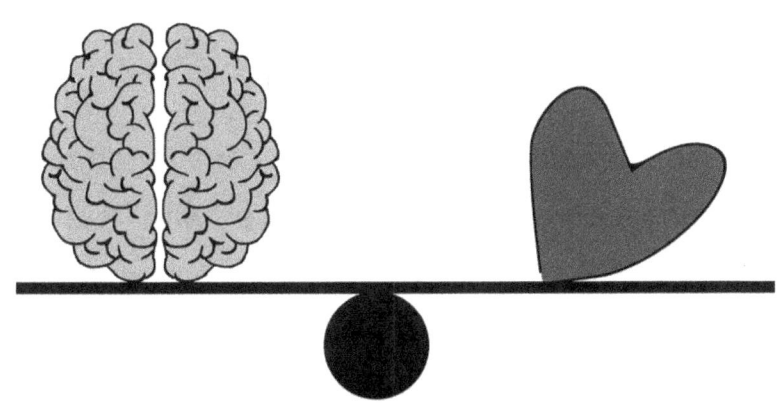

Emotions are the mental state in line with feelings that change how a person behaves and their judgments towards different people, situations or events. Emotions alter the normal feelings of a person depending on their current mental state. These emotions include hate, anger, love, depression, loneliness, excitement, embarrassment, pride and shame.

Scientifically, emotions are connected to the nerves that determine how we feel and think about people, situations and events. They dictate our movements, actions and every single idea that we make. Our relationship with other people is determined by the state of our emotions. Sometimes communication becomes difficult when we are not in the right state of emotions and when everything is well, communication becomes better.

Emotions influence a person's personality and have a great impact on how they relate with others. It determines their interpretation of events and actions. People respond differently to every action and how their responses are normally contributed to by their current state of emotions. How a person feels towards a particular event or another person can never be the same way we all think about them. Our different feelings and opinions are always as a result of the different emotions.

Overexcitement can make someone overreact, overpromise or do something in excess that will spoil the fun of it. Sometimes it makes a person and forgets something important that will cost them in the future. This usually happens as a result of being too much obsessed about an event or situation that takes away your mind and focus it all towards a single event. You are subjected to doing things beyond normal when you get too much excited about something.

A person can also underestimate or overestimate something depending on their level of excitement. Excitement is the key determinant of our judgment and reaction towards everything. It makes us to either judge so low or too high based on how it makes us feel about the situation or person. It can make us have an excess urge of doing something or lose interest in it completely.

Depression, as well as a state of emotions, determines how we feel, how we act and our response to different reactions and also how we perceive things. Someone who is depressed is subjected to always seeing the negative out of everything. They in most circumstances attend to compare everything that happens to then to what they had experienced in the past that led to that state of mind. It makes them think that nothing is worth being happy for. They are made to believe that only made things are meant for them and that nothing good can happen to their life that will ever make them feel like other people.

Post-Traumatic stress also makes a person to fear facing life as it is. They are scared of trying something new for the fear of landing in the same state that they were in before. Maybe this person was involved in an accident that killed all other passengers leaving him or her as the only survivor of the scenario. The scene that they witnessed will ever be fresh in their mind that any time they want to travel, they will always have the fear of getting involved in a fatal accident. Some victims end up refusing to ever travel and this is all because of fear and trauma that never ends.

Some people after surviving an accident that killed many people are always left feeling guilty of themselves. They normally think that it was their fault that many died but they survived. They carry in their heart a burden that they should not carry because they don't deserve it. Guilt affects the mental state of any normal person making them think too much about a situation that it even becomes harmful to their health. These kind of people are always fragile to any kind of attack and generally, appear weak all the time.

Someone can also be traumatized after losing something that meant a lot to them. A person can lose a lot of money through theft or a failed business. This will leave these victims subjected to too much stress that they never planned for. They will be thinking of how to recover their lost money but will be afraid to invest again for the fear of losing for yet another time. This kind of emotional stress affects many people that even lead to them not focusing on their goals and are taken many steps behind.

Curiosity also makes a person think constantly of a particular thing that they are always in a hurry to know more about it. They can go to an extreme extent without thinking of the danger involved. Their minds are taken away out of this state of emotions and the only thing they think about is knowing more about a particular event, where it took place and when and even how it happened. If they don't get someone to give them full information of whatever it is that they are anxious about, they feel so incomplete and the constant struggle to gather the full information about it can even lead them to some kind of trouble that they never expected and that could have been avoided if only they let go of that particular event.

A person can usually feel so lonely that they attempt to think that no one in the society wants to be around them and that they don't deserve to be treated in a better way. This emotional state makes many people start distancing themselves from other people and prefer to spend time away from other people and also keep their thoughts and ideas to themselves. Such people are never ready to share how they feel even if they need help. They will always choose to keep everything to themselves and this is because they normally fear no one will be ready to listen to them or give solutions to their worries.

Being so lonely can make a person start thinking of odd things that are sometimes dangerous to them or other people. Some people will think of taking away their lives because they will think that they are leaving a useless life and that they have no reason to stay alive. This sometimes occurs as a result of pressure from work, school or from within the family. These people will feel so isolated and unfit in society that is full of different kind of people from different backgrounds.

Having low self-esteem makes a person feel so rejected and very weird of themselves. Their failure to see their worth and think that other people are more important than them and that their living standards are so low as compared to how other people live their lives. They start comparing themselves with others and feel bad every time they fail to achieve what others have achieved. What they normally forget and that is very important is that their destination is far much different from the destinations of other people and that there are always different routes that lead to the same destination. They don't realize that they don't have to do exactly what others do to lead a better life as them and that everything takes time. They can never start and finish at the same time.

Some emotions lead a person to hate other people and events to an extent that there can never stand the thought of them. They are dragged by their emotions to think that these people or events are a disgrace to them and a threat to their happiness. They can never bear the feeling of being around these people and whenever they come around them, they are made to either walk away or treat them with silence and wrath. They are so much annoyed by the fact that they have to be around such people. Any single mistake that these people make appear to them as the worst mistake ever and that does not deserve to be forgiven. They will keep talking about it over and over again to express how bad they feel towards the people that are involved.

Hatred can make a person overreact towards anything that is done by the person they don't like. They become too cross with these people's opinions that they never calm down to give them a listening ear. Everything done or said by these people disgust them too much and none of their ideas is never right according to them. They think of the other person as the worst enemy all the time and they never think of making up for things to work well between them.

Anger is also influenced by emotions. It makes a person feel so bitter towards something that offends them. It normally leads to fights that become difficult to control and reconcile. If anger is not well handled, it can lead to a person saying hurting words that can never be retracted or doing things that can never be undone but leaves a scar that is never-ending on someone's heart. Some people murder because of anger and some kill themselves. However, emotionally intelligent people will always find it easy to control their emotions to manage their anger and avoid things that cost them a lifetime to forget.

Anger can destroy the relationship between friends, family, and colleagues when someone overreacts to a given event. Not everyone will be in a position to control their emotions and change how they feel about something that has already happened. It takes a lot of maturity and courage to handle things calmly without hurting other people's feelings or making them feel unwanted.

Emotions driven by anxiety makes a person be too much alert and expects anything to happen anytime. They bring curiosity and fear in a person that they can never relax and feel normal all the time. They always believe that something must happen whether good or bad. The mentally that something must happen is what makes some people go insane. This is because they tend to have the fear of experiencing a bad situation that may affect their mental status and distract their brains.

Emotions are connected to the nerves that direct our feelings. The nerves signal the brain about an event that is just about to take place or that is already taking place. How the brain responds to the alarm of the nerves with determining how we will react to that event. It allows us to either react positively or negatively depending on the signal that the brain receives. A feeling that supply bitter signals to the brain resulting in negative reactions and thoughts.

Someone can feel embarrassed by something which will make them afraid and uncomfortable around other people. They won't be able to interact freely as they used to before and facing situations becomes difficult to them. They are controlled by the result of what they did that did not turn out as they expected or as was expected by the people who interact with them.Taking about that thing in their presence makes them feel so bad and unfit.

Embarrassment also lowers a person's confidence in what they are doing. They think that everything they do will turn out imperfect making other people to underrate their ability. It makes them do everything unwillingly or filled with doughnuts about their ability and the far they can go if they focus much on their duties and responsibilities without recalling something that had happened and cannot be retrieved.

To understand how emotions work, you first need to understand the possible causes of emotions. Emotions are normally a result of our own thoughts. They occur from the experiences that we get involved in our day to day life activities. It is true that we do encounter different experiences from different situations that may have involved several people. According to scientists, many people may be involved in a similar event but this will impact different emotions in them usually because of the different thoughts that are involved in each of them.

These can be noticed anywhere maybe in school, in church, at work or at home. It may involve your coworkers, family or friends. For an instant, imagine a situation where two or three people have a walk together then you happen to come across a dog. One person can feel scared at the thought that this dog can be harmful and maybe scream or run away from it. This is a feeling that is usually experienced by someone who had never had a pet dog earlier. On the other hand, the other person will get attracted to the dog and admire its appearance. This person may comment "oh, this dog is so cute." This is common with people who grew up with the mentality of pet dogs in their lives. This brings out a picture of different people with different experiences having different thoughts and ideas of the same event.

People attempt to think differently about different events and other people. These different thoughts can result in different feelings and changes in what the body does, what you think about or get interested in, what action you want to take and how you respond to different reactions. These different changes are what we use to figure out our feelings and emotions.

Scientists say that different state of thoughts will definitely lead to a different state of emotions. For example, when someone thinks "I have failed exams" that person will normally panic and feel some sense of fear within them. Someone who thinks "I have made it" will probably feel so happy and excited while a person who thinks they have been wronged or badly threatened by other people will automatically feel angry and anxious.

Thoughts that are leading to different emotions always have different questions involved like;

- Did it happen as per the expectations
- Is it worth celebrating
- What is its impact on what I wanted to achieve
- Will it lead me to what I wanted or take me a step backward
- What will happen next
- Am I in a position to control what will follow
- Do I have the ability to endure what has already taken place
- Who's the fault is it that this particular situation was encountered

Anything that happens will call for different feelings and emotions depending on your mind and thoughts and how you will interpret and respond to these questions. For example, if you business fails or gets robbed, you will definitely feel sad if you are not sure you can have a solution to it or invest in a different way to recover what you have lost. You will feel so depressed and think that this is the end of everything for you. However, someone else may quickly think of a possible solution, maybe an insurance cover that they had taken before and feel relieved because this kind of event will not have severe impact on their business, or, they will strike out a plan for a different and alternative way of investing the little cash they are left with that will be more profitable to cover up for the loss they had experienced.

You can also feel sad when you lose someone you were so attached to and have never imagined being away from them. Maybe you broke up with your partner after being in a relationship for so many years. You may feel so worried about this particular situation and find it unbearable and hard for you to let go. You will get stack at the thought of having lost the best person in your life and moving on will be such a hard task for you. This situation can impact different feelings in your heart. You may be filled with so much hatred that you do not feel like falling in love anymore. You may find yourself having a totally negative attitude towards the opposite sex right from the experience that you got involved in.

In some situations, you can encounter some emotions but you don't have even a single idea as to why you feel so. Sometimes you will feel some emotions but you will not be in a position to notice any thoughts that can result in such kind of emotions. Understanding this situation can sometimes be hard. However, it is said that sometimes your brain can signal an emotion out of unconsciousness. This implies that our brains might trigger an emotional reaction to something they have noticed about our situations but we might totally have no idea about this and we can never notice it. The scientist has found out that our brains get involved in so many activities that we never notice.

When emotions are triggered, the brain changes the body us doing too much the emotions. For example, when you are overexcited about something, the speed of your heartbeat will increase and you will feel so nervous. The same apple when you feel so scared and afraid. You become so uncomfortable and feel uneasy all the time.

People can also think differently at the same time. For example, someone can be happy but find themselves around another person who is so sad. The sad person will normally think about the sad situations in the past that match their current feelings and think that nothing good will ever happen to make them happy while in the other hand, the person who is happy will only think of what they can do to enjoy themselves or some past situations that ever made them feel so happy and they would like to bring it back to their lives one more time so that they get to feel the same for another time.

The different thoughts and feelings are signaled by our brains that make the muscles to react differently making us to either smile, shed tears or have a frowned faces. When we learn to balance our thoughts, balancing our emotions becomes easy as well. Emotions and thoughts go hand in hand with each other. When we have negative thoughts, we will only have negative emotions and positive thoughts result in positive emotions.

Emotions push us to do weird things and act differently from how we normally act. For example, emotions can make you want to destroy something completely or hit someone so hard when you are angry. You can also fee as you should really run away whenever you feel scared or distance yourself from other people when you are sad. You will only want to be left alone to think about yourself and everything that is happening to you. Everyone will seem like a bother to you whenever they try to be close to you or talk to you.

When a person is happy, they will always have an excess urge of jumping here and there or talking to anyone that they come across. Emotions make them to badly want to do something that is not normal or that to engage in activities that they do not usually engage in. Their feelings are ever beyond the normal feelings of a normal person.

It is normal for a person to be unsure of what they are feeling. This is because at times our emotions and feelings tend to be so confusing and need too much time and effort to understand. The same kind of emotions can subject different feelings in different events, while different types of emotions can subject to similar feelings towards a given situation. This leaves everyone wondering what has come over them and how they can control it. However, controlling this mental state is never easy since at times you don't even realize when your brain triggers some types of feelings and emotions.

When you come to realize you are experiencing and emotional reaction, you still have an added task of figuring out what it is that you are feeling and why. For example when you go to a neighbor who has a pet, when the pet dog looks at you your heart might start racing and you will think that the emotions you ate feeling is fear. You will easily think that you are undergoing fear because you are afraid this dog can hurt you. However, is such situations, some people will act strong and courageous that they don't feel the fear of being hurt by the pet dog. Their emotions will react differently from those of a person that has never been used to being around pet dogs.

I have come across a number of people who get their relatives and friends admitted to a hospital. Most f these people are always filled with the fear of losing their relatives and friends to the hands of death. They are taken away with panic and anxiety that they even start thinking of how life will be without these people. They allow their minds to imagine that these people are gone already and start fantasizing the kind of life they will live without the people they were used to and that they cherished too much.

On the other hand, others are always hopeful that their loved ones will recover and be with them again. They think positively about the situation and keep praying to God that these people get well soon and join them in living a normal life that is free from sickness and pain. When these people do not recover, their friends and families are left traumatized and filled with regret. Some people will think that it is their fault that this situation came along and Starr blaming themselves for not being in a position to stop everything from happening the way it happened. This traumatizes the people involved in leaving their minds occupied by too much stress about the situation.

Not everyone is in a position to figure out what they feel towards something and this has been proven by scientists. They again extend it and say that a person who does not find it easy to figure out how they feel and understand their emotions does not have to struggle to make themselves feel comfortable. It is ever easy for them to feel better at any time. Unlike the others who can easily tell what they are feeling. It makes it difficult for them to come out of the situation and feel better.

Paying close attention to your emotions is very important. It helps you to start practicing how to figure out what you are feeling and how you can come out of it with much ease. When you train yourself this way, it will be easy for you to overcome a difficult situation and feel better whenever you are down. It makes healing easier and faster and also helps you to understand what you have learned from different situations when you felt angry, sad or anxious. Handling similar situations in the future becomes easier when you get to deal with them from the start.

Understanding your emotions comes with a lot of advantages. It helps you figure out how you can overcome different situations without feeling so awkward and weak. It also helps you figure out how you can respond to your emotions in different situations by helping you to tell whether your current emotions much the current situation and if not, what can you do about it to balance it with the situation.

Emotional reactions sometimes become helpful in some events. For example, when a child sees fire and gets scared of getting close to it. The fear of not going around a fireplace will help to prevent the child from getting burnt. Also in a situation where someone goes out with their friends and see other people swim in the ocean but they are scared of getting into the water to swim with them. That fear helps to protect them from being drowned or getting attacked by ocean animals.

Lastly, someone who fears to invest in forex trade for the first time will protect themselves from the risk of losing their capital.

However, when these emotions happen in the wrong situation, they become unhelpful. For example when you get mad at your boss because they corrected you over something that you did not do according to their expectations. This can make you quit your job or get fired when you react rudely to them. This only leads to a loss instead of again. Or when you are scared of asking a question in class to get more clarification about a point that is mentioned by your lecturer. This will hinder you from getting the information you need and you might end up failing a test just because you were afraid of asking a question in class.

It is good to listen to what your emotions are telling you if it so helpful but you can also dodge your emotions and reorganize your thoughts when they are unhelpful and likely to cause trouble. For example, when you feel affected by what your boss or colleague said, you can rethink about your job and assume them to protect your job or think of an alternative way of earning then quit that particular job. Also when you are afraid of asking a question in class during an ongoing lecture, you can opt for consulting a different lecturer who is familiar with that field or your fellow student who understood better what was taught.

Some emotions can be controlled by exercise or activities. For example, when you are angry, you can engage yourself in activities like swimming, jogging or take a walk. These activities will help you feel relaxed and let go of the anger that was previously burning within you. You will feel relieved and let go of the past situation that made you feel so angry. Sadness can also be controlled easily by engaging in some activities. When you sit home alone and think of past sad experience all the time, you will never get over it. You will always feel so low and depressed but when you get out and get yourself involved in different activities, you will be able to come back to your normal state of mind and let go of what happened that made you sad.

Going out to spend time with friends is also another way of healing from negative emotions. It helps you forget the sad event by distracting your mind through the conversations that you hold with friends. For an instant, when you get invited to a party, you make up your mind to go out and join your friends to party with them. You would have freed yourself from the circle of thinking about the past situation and getting hurt more by more. You will feel some sort of joy and positive feelings within you.

Emotions can control a person's decisions when we allow them to overpower us. We can become prisoners of our own emotions when we let emotions control what we do all the time. Look at a situation where you feel angry at your sibling. You can be highly tempered and fight them back. What if this fight leads to one person getting injured, or you hit a sensitive place and kill your brother. You will have involved yourself in another difficult situation that you did not plan for and that you would have avoided if you did not allow yourself to be controlled by harsh emotions.

Emotions are triggered by the brain but should be managed by us immediately we realize that we are in a state of emotions that is dangerous to us and to those around us. It can be difficult to deal with the emotions if you don't understand them and cannot figure out how it is and how to come over it. You will be left stranded between decisions and if you don't make the right choice then you are doomed.

Emotions are manipulative. If they take over us, they attempt to dictate our actions and responses towards different reactions. Emotions can make you do something that you would not have done if you were in the right state of mind. It can influence you to hate someone for no good reason and only see the worst in them despite their struggles to make things straight. Negative emotions will only make you think of doing something negative without thinking of the possible results.

Emotions can lead to revenge a bad action with the same treatment. This will gain you nothing but only lead you to problems and make things worse for you. Coming out of a bad experience that was influenced by your own emotions is not an easy task. You will have struggle and fight your thoughts to feel normal and if you can't come out of it, your emotions will still suggest negative solutions to you. Things like running away from home or committing suicide or even killing someone who makes you feel bad.

Emotions disturb our minds and increase our passion for something that we have in mind. They can impose conflict in our mind trying to overcome a bad feeling or trying to avoid a particular event to prevent something from happening. People who are led by their emotions are always in trouble trying to go against their own feelings to save the situation. Having to do everything as dictated by your emotions only makes you a slave of your own thoughts. It becomes more burden to us than anything else.

Emotions can make someone too possessed with another person or event. This normally occurs in the event of relationships. You can be too much into someone that you don't see their faults at all. Anything they do will sound right according to you and no one can ever convince you that some wrong is happening to your relationship because you chose to trust your emotions too much to an extent of giving up your happiness for the sake of your partner.

Remember your partner have emotions too and when they realize that you are too much into them that you can't avoid them at any cost, their emotions will lead them to take advantage of your feelings for them and use you to achieve what they have been longing for over a very long time. You will have no choice but to serve their interests because you have allowed yourself to fall in the trap of your own emotions and the manipulative emotions of your partner.

Scientists have discovered that emotions take over someone if they are not strong enough to stand against them. They control every single decision that these people make leading them to a destination that they never prepared for. This can make a person do several things unknowingly and only realize it when they are already in trouble with other things. It disorients their minds leading to failure of plans that would have been productive and profitable.

Emotions are the worst rulers of a person's mind. Psychologists have said that most mentally unstable people are always victims of their own emotions. They are controlled by their negative emotions to destroy things and put the blame on someone else. Or, they are forced to get too much affected by the absence of something in their life that they can never have peace without that thing or person but again when they get what they want, they attempt to misuse them under the influence of these negative emotions that can never be controlled by them.

Such people in most cases end up losing more than they gain. It is because their emotions make them want to start away from other people and because of their bad attitude towards other people, most people also attempt to avoid interacting with them to stay away from troubles that are always caused by these people. Their emotions take full control of them and people are made to believe that they are insane even if they are not.

Children are easily affected by their emotions and those of the people around them. If their emotions make them believe that a particular thing can hurt them, they will be convinced that it is dangerous for them to be found around such things and the fear of getting hurt will always keep them away. It will be difficult to make them believe that they can be around these things without getting hurt. What their own emotions tell them can never be taken away by anyone.

Children too when they observe a negative attitude towards them in someone much older than them, they will be scared of interacting with this person. They fear of being treated harshly will make them avoid this person by all the possible means. No one can ever come between them and their thoughts to convince them that this person cannot hurt them. They are highly affected by the thought of being involved with the person that they are scared of.

Emotions control even the toughest people. For example, when it is announced that terrorists are attacking people in a given region within your country, and you happen to be in the region or someone who is very close to you is within that region. You will be filled with the fear of you getting attacked or your friends or family members. This fear will eat over your mind making you become restless all the time.

Someone who is not in that region will also be scared of going to that region for the fear of getting involved in the terror attack. They are driven by the emotions of fear to believe that if they get to that region they will never be spared of the attack. They fear losing their lives can even lead to some people being helplessly depressed.

People who happen to witness a terror attack or human slaughter, or just get to watch the clips of such events are exposed to the trauma of what the saw. They develop fear within them that gets them scared all the time. Such people are exposed to weak and fragile personalities that they can't even stand simple jokes that are relating to such events. These people are driven by their emotions to get scared of anything.

They can panic at the sight of any even that raises attention.

According to scientific studies and proves, emotions do not choose anyone's personality. Everyone has a nervous system that is connected to the brain. Once the responsible nerves signal the brain of a particular situation, the brain will trigger the related emotions before you realize it. The impact of this emotion in someone's reactions will depend on their psychology and emotional experience. Someone who is emotionally week will automatically follow the commands of their emotions and end up doing something that was not their intention.

On the other end, a person who studied and understand the psychology of emotions will find it easy to change their thoughts and go for an alternative way of overcoming the situation without causing any trouble. They can never react according to their emotions when they understand that the resulting situation may affect them negatively or inconvenience other people. They will divert their attention to a possible and positive solution even if it means they have to go against their own emotions.

People who are psychologically stable have active mind control techniques to control their mind and those of other people. These people can easily detect manipulative emotions within them or in the people that they interact with. This will direct them on how to apply the mind control techniques to prevent these emotions from negatively ruling the situation. They can then come up with a positive solution that makes everyone fill good about the situation.

Emotions are two-phased and can either result in something positive or the opposite of what was expected. They can help us come out of the trap when we use them carefully but again when they come the opposite way, they can land us into trouble and even spoil our relationship with others.

Chapter 2: How to Control and Change Emotions through Emotional Intelligence Concepts

A Comprehensive Definition of Emotional Intelligence

Emotional intelligence is also referred to as emotional quotient (EQ). This is the ability of understanding, using and managing your emotions in a positive way. This is meant to relieve oneself from stress, be able to effectively communicate, to overcome challenges, show empathy to others and defusing conflicts. Emotional intelligence can be of great need in building stronger relationships, achievement of personal goals and in career, and also succeeding at work and at school. Apart from that, it can also assist you in connecting with feelings, turning intentions into actions and even making informed decisions.

Attributes that defines Emotional Intelligence

The following are some attributes that are commonly used to define emotional intelligence:

- **Self-awareness**

This entails you identifying your own emotions and the effects that they have on your behavior and thoughts. This will, therefore, help you to realize where your weaknesses and strengths lie thus gain self-confidence.

- **Relationship management**

This entails you know the way you can develop and also maintain a perfect relationship, inspire, communicate clearly, influence others, manage conflict and also be able to work well with a team.

- **Social awareness**

This basically refers to you having empathy towards others. You can, therefore, be able to understand other people's needs, concerns, and even emotions. You will also be able to understand the various emotional cues and pick up on them, have a comfortable social status and also recognizing the power of change in an organization or a group.

- **Self-management**

This refers to your own ability to manage impulsive behaviors and feelings. It also entails managing your own emotions in good approaches, adapting to the changing circumstances and following up commitments.

Benefits of Teaching Emotional Intelligence in Schools

As children and teens develop and grow, emotional intelligence is very vital. Much evidence has been put up to demonstrate how it positively helps students to handle stressful conditions, be comfortable during transitions they face and even develop relationships with other students.

Knowledge of emotional intelligence is very important to students especially those who are still in their teenage. It helps students to effectively employ emotions to be productive in their studies and adapt to the school system without going through many challenges.

The following are a few benefits that students will gain by having this knowledge at hand:
- Students will improve and achieve more in their academics.
- Students will learn and gain active listening skills.
- Students will be self-aware thus know their capabilities.

In the recent past, emotional intelligence studies have been so popular among teens and generally students. One of the critical ideas is that emotional intelligence should be incorporated into the school curriculum and not isolated. This, therefore, means that there has been more focus on the way in which we can put more focus on social and emotional learning. This program will help schools to have the emotional intelligence principles in their curriculum. Through the coaching of students, teacher training and other resources such as evidence-based, emotional intelligence will be taught at all levels of studies. This will be of great help to students as they will be able to know the skills and approaches needed to manage and change their emotions. As a result of this, the job market in the near future will be flooded with the brilliant mind of people who are capable of dealing with stressful conditions in the workplace.

These are people who will also have a good relationship and achieve many successes in their lives both professionally or even personally.

Importance of Emotional Intelligence

Emotional Intelligence is linked to various aspects in one's life if not all. It can, therefore, be said that it can be linked to our careers, job performance, and even our success. The following are, therefore, the various ways which have depicted the importance of emotional intelligence:

- **Emotional Intelligence and Job Performance**

In the recent past, there has been a rise in emotional intelligence awareness in management-focused literature together with leadership training summits. This gives us an indication that there exists a very strong relationship between job performance and emotional intelligence. It not only proves to exist but also has depicted an array of value in different areas.

One's workplace is a representation of a social community that is very separate from their personal lives. This is also a place where increased appreciation of emotional intelligence has been on the rise allowing people to have an understanding of themselves and even others, be conversant with hard situations and communicating in a more effective manner. This, therefore, means that employing emotional intelligence at your workplace might greatly improve your personal and even other individuals' social capabilities.

Emotional Intelligence entails management of emotions which improves job performance, which in turn helps people to stay calm and think logically thus establishing good working relationships and achievement of goals. Apart from that, there is an evident relationship between emotional intelligence and how senior employees manage their juniors. A manager who has got a high emotional intelligence is well conversant with the stress management skills and also how recognize and manage the stress in other people. Therefore, if we put emotional intelligence in the stress management perspective, then the relationship between job performance and emotional intelligence is crystal clear. This is because one's commitment to their job is highly and positively impacted by stress management.

In many instances, emotional intelligence usually applies to all kinds of employees and not only those at the management level. The employees that are at the lower rank in the hierarchy of an organization and have a high emotional intelligence usually have got desires and abilities to establish and maintain good relationships at the workplace. Apart from that, these individuals are good in management and resolution of conflicts. This, therefore, means that they have the capability of sustaining relationships that exists in the workplace as compared to those with either low or moderate emotional intelligence.

In the current job market, many organizations are undergoing revolution and changes in different sectors. This has made organizations to have the need of employees who can easily cope up with these changes and respond to them easily. This indicates that emotional intelligence is an important factor in job performance in both group and individual levels. This thus clearly describes the way in which emotional intelligence is of value.

- **Emotional Intelligence and Resilience**

Emotional intelligence has proved to be a valuable tool in adversity as it has the potential of enhancing not only teamwork effectiveness and leadership abilities but it is also an important tool in enhancing personal resilience. The impact of emotional intelligence on the resilience of a person is the ability of that person to cope up with situations that are stressful. It has been clearly demonstrated by research that a person who has got high emotional intelligence usually easily overcome stressors and their negative impacts.

Focusing on leadership, a leader is usually expected to have increased responsibilities which usually are accompanied by potential stressors. In such a case, it is important for the person to have strong emotional intelligence in order to be resilient and battle with these stressful conditions.

From research where investigations were done into the link existing between emotional intelligence and stress, it was found out that people who showed high emotional intelligence levels were not negatively affected by stressors. These participants did an emotional intelligence ability-based test before the threat level that was posed by the two stressors was rated. After that, they reported their emotional reactions the stressors before being subjected to physiological stress to also assess their responses. The findings of this research showed that emotional intelligence has a relationship with lower threats. This study, therefore, provides us with a valid prediction that stress resilience is facilitated by emotional intelligence.

From further research done, the relationship between high levels of emotional intelligence, the tendency to depressive behaviors and resilience was drawn. It was found out that there was a positive correlation that exists between mindfulness, self-compassion, and resilience with the rate of burnout. In conclusion, individuals who have got high emotional intelligence levels were more resilient and could not easily fall into depression or burnout.

Emotional intelligence has a strong link to the individual's advancement and also their performance. Evidence also suggests that there is a significant link between their resilience and their motivation to achieve. Apart from that, it also made a suggestion that resilience acts as a mediator between self-motivated achievement and resilience. Resilience, in this case, has got a perseverance component that acts as a motivation to motivation when facing obstacles.

From the various research findings and theories, we have seen a strong relationship between emotional intelligence and resilience. We have clearly seen how one's emotional intelligence levels affect their resilience. This, therefore, has proved emotional intelligence to be very important.

- **Emotional Intelligence and Motivation**

Emotional intelligence is one of the key ingredients for motivation which in turn is very vital in the achievement of success. An emotionally intelligent person will always have an understanding of what they aspire and the necessary motivation skills that they would need to achieve these aspirations. There are four elements that are said to make up motivation; how we commit ourselves to the goals we set, how ready we are to utilize opportunities, self-drive to improve and how resilient we are.

Motivation is said to be a psychological process that which we use to psyche ourselves into action in order to realize a desirable outcome. It doesn't matter the action we are doing, whether dedication of much time to work on a project or just changing the TV channel using a remote, without being motivated we cannot act.

This is because motivation energizes, arouses, sustains and directs performance and behavior. The motivation that usually comes from within, also known as intrinsic motivation usually drives us to the achievement of our full capability. A person who is emotionally intelligent has got both skills required to motivate themselves and those needed to motivate other people too. This is a very useful skill to possess especially if you are in a management position in your job.

Self-motivation is the key to the achievement of one's goals. With self-motivation, emotionally intelligent people will always be capable of impacting the motivation of employees. The ability to determine the emotions and needs or concerns of others is a great skill to possess in relation to the determination of perfect methods of motivating individuals and teams.

From a study and research did, it was found out that the emotional intelligence of a first-year graduate was positively linked to their self-motivation to studying the respective course and choosing that course. Another study of senior employees with very high emotional intelligence found out that they are good in arguments, have good behavior and great work outcomes. It, therefore, means that a happy employee is a motivated employee.

The capability to be conversant with anxiety and stress is a very useful emotional intelligence tool when it comes to motivation. From the above studies and research findings, it is clear that emotional intelligence plays a major role in one's motivation. Since motivation is a very vital tool in our actions, then emotional intelligence is also very important.

- **Emotional Intelligence and Decision-Making**

Emotional intelligence plays a key role in both professional and personal development. It not only has an impact on the way in which we handle our behaviors and control our social complexities but also the approaches we take in decision-making. Having an in-depth understanding of the emotions you feel and the reason as to why you are feeling them can heavily impact your decision-making capabilities. This, therefore, means that if we carefully look into our emotions, then we can avoid making misleading and misguided decisions.

Emotional intelligence is a very vital tool required in the prevention of making poor decisions based on our emotions whereby lower emotional intelligence can make you anxious and result in you making a poor misguided decision. This does not mean that we should keep emotions aside when making decisions but discovering these emotions which might not have any relationship with the problem and ensuring that they do not influence the decision that you are going to make.

Negative emotions can be a stumbling block to decision making and problem-solving in either your workplace or even personal circumstances. Being able to recognize emotions that are becoming a stumbling block to making rational decisions and being able to effectively ignore the emotions will prevent their negative influence on your decision. This, therefore, means that decision making at this stage will be much favored as it will not be negatively influenced in any way.

From research done through observations and administering a series of questions, it was discovered that people and organizations reaped big benefits from a practical application of emotional intelligence in making decisions. This study had the aim of improving emotional intelligence awareness and how emotional intelligence skills can be employed in decision making. From the observations, it was discovered that having training sessions on emotional intelligence is one of the most effective ways to incorporate decision-making skills and also helps you to understand the possible consequences of poor decision-making.

Having an understanding of the causes and possible consequences of emotions gives you the freedom to manage and make a decision about the feeling. For instance, if you have an argument with your spouse the go to work without resolving it you will probably stay angry the whole day. Being angry at work, your colleague might make an offer to you but you dismiss it without even paying attention to it. This is a kind of emotional interference that can be very dangerous to your decision-making. If you have high emotional intelligence, then you can be able to identify this form of emotional interference and manage it thus avoiding making decisions that are emotionally driven. This, therefore, means that emotional intelligence is vital when making decisions.

- **Emotional Intelligence and Success**

There are things which mean different to different people. As happiness is so is a success which everyone has a different version of defining it. But no matter no success is defined, it is clear that emotional intelligence plays an important part in its achievement. From history, most intelligent individuals are usually not attributed to greatest successes. This is because IQ is not sufficient on its own to enable one to succeed in life. In regards to this, you can be the most intelligent person but if you lack emotional quotient, you may fail to turn down people with negative thoughts about you and even manage stress. This shows that emotional intelligence is sometimes even more powerful as compared to IQ in life success.

Your emotional intelligence is the actual thing that helps you to achieve your life objectives and realize great successes. Therefore, developing emotional intelligence would influence your achievements through contribution to your morale, cooperation and most importantly motivation by a great margin. In a workplace, the managers and employees who perform well as compared to others usually employ strategies that are associated with emotional intelligence in the management of conflicts, reduction of stress and thus achieving their goals.

In the recent past, there has been blooming evidence of a range of activities said to constitute emotional intelligence are now vital in determining success. This refers to success both in the workplace and also one's personal life. It incorporates applications that we associate with in our daily lives in relationships, businesses, and even parenting. Emotional intelligence guides one to easily manage their emotions in situations that are likely to provoke anxiety. These situations include when taking examinations at the university. It is also positively associated with success in social functioning and personal relationships.

In social relationships, success achievable with the employment of emotional intelligence skills to determine other people's emotions, then adopt their emotional states and thus regulate the way they behave. This briefly shows how important emotional intelligence is in achieving success in the different spheres of life.

- **Emotional Intelligence and Communication**

One's ability to have the knowledge and understanding of their emotions might aid them to be aware and understand the feelings that other people are experiencing. This has got an impact on the way in which we communicate in our daily lives.

Considering communication in conflict resolution in the workplace, people with great emotional intelligence levels would most probably approach the conflict in the most reasonable way possible and negotiate together with others to finally come up with a reasonable outcome. On the contrary, a person with lower levels of emotional intelligence will not be able to solve the conflict in a reasonable calm manner thus might even end up without a solution at the end.

In the workplace, relationships are usually affected by the manner in which we can manage our emotions and also understanding the emotions of those around us. The capability to do this helps us in communicating without necessarily resorting to confrontation. If you have high emotional intelligence, then it is beyond doubt that you are equipped with conflict management skills and thus you will be able to put up a meaningful relationship guaranteed capacity to understand and address needs of those they engage with.

In recent years, emotional intelligence has been able to receive much attention that drives effective communication within individuals and even teams. On close examination of emotional intelligence as a reason for team success, you will find that it does not only do it drives the viability of a team but also affects communication quality in a positive way.

Achievement of successful communication in relation to successful negotiation and conflict has a very close relationship with high emotional intelligence levels. In this case, individuals with lower emotional intelligence would be so defensive in such stressful situations. This will instead escalate the conflict instead of managing it. If you have high emotional intelligence, then this means that you have got the necessary skills to ensure effective communication without resulting in a confrontation. From this, we can easily derive the importance and great contribution that high levels of emotional intelligence add to the achievement of effective communication.

- **Emotional Intelligence and Happiness**

Just like any other word or felling, happiness seems something easy but actually getting to understand it is when you will realize that it is a hard nut to crack. This is because different people have got different instances and experiences that they describe them to mean happiness to them. Truly, happiness means different to different people but undoubtedly, emotional intelligence is a great requirement to have despite the kind of interpretation you prefer. Happiness is an emotional intelligence facilitator that contributes to each and everyone's self-actualization which positively impacts our happiness.

From a study where the relationship between different interpersonal relations and emotional intelligence was examined, it was discovered that individuals with high emotional intelligence scored highly in self-monitoring, social skills and taking empathic perspective. Apart from that, they also scored highly in affectionate relationships, satisfaction in relationships, and cooperation with their partners.

Emotional intelligence skills are very important when it comes to reducing stress, thus, in turn, will positively impact on one's happiness and wellbeing in general. Apart from the motivational value that it possesses, happiness acts as a monitor to the wellbeing of an individual. It is also a source of a positive mood to the manner in which the person copes up and meets daily needs, pressures and challenges.

Positivity is what actually encourages the emotional energy required in the increment of an individual's motivational levels which is responsible for getting things done. It actually helps one to be successful in what they are doing and even gets to the extent of telling them the extent of success they are actually achieving.

From a study done by Furnham, it was realized that a large section of variance that is evident in the wellbeing and happiness of a person is determined by their emotional intelligence levels. This refers to their ability to stabilize their emotions, social competence, and even relationship skills. Although these emotional intelligence skills are not the only source of one's happiness, it is very vital to realize that they contribute and impacts our happiness up to 50%. This, therefore, prove it to be a very vital thing which should always be put into consideration.

Happiness has, therefore, proven to be closely linked to emotional intelligence if the research and studies detailed above are to go by. A person with high emotional intelligence will have the necessary skills to dodge any obstructions that might act as a hindrance to happiness. On the other hand, a person who has low levels of emotional intelligence will not be able to cope up with these obstructions and end up always sad and stressed up. This thus proves emotional intelligence to be vital.

- **Emotional Intelligence and Goals**

In life, each and every person has got goals and achievements that they hope to achieve someday in life. In order to achieve these goals, there are various conditions that usually impact it either positively or negatively. In this case, emotional intelligence also plays a key role in the achievement of these goals. Emotional intelligence will drive you to realize self-actualization which requires you to first get motivated.

In order to have the motivation, you will need to be happy with whatever you do. This is because lack of happiness will challenge you in pursuit of the motivational levels that are required to achieve your goals.

In order to realize success and eventually achieve your dreams and goals, there is a need to employ emotional intelligence skills. If you have high emotional intelligence levels, you will definitely perform excellently in what you are doing in all aspects. The effectiveness of a person or a team in a certain process directly reflects their emotional intelligence skill level. Those with high emotional intelligence levels will perform well while those with lower intelligence levels would perform dismally and might never achieve their goals.

If we want to produce best results in what we do and achieve the goals we might have set, then all we need is a positive self-regard, effective skills to solve problems, skills to make informed decisions and informed self-awareness. All these are directly attributed to one's emotional intelligence. This, therefore, means that our levels of emotional intelligence dictate if we will achieve our goals or not.

Low emotional intelligence will see you fail and never achieve the set goals. On the other hand, high emotional intelligence levels with required emotional skills are very important and they will positively contribute to the achievement of your goals in life.

How to Control and Change Emotions through Emotional Intelligence Concepts

In life generally, we go through diverse situations that might sometimes arouse emotions within us. Being emotional is also not a good thing as such but if we can be able to change and control our emotions in these situations, then we are better off. There are various approaches that can be employed to effectively manage the emotions that we experience. Among these approaches is the emotional intelligence concepts which are very ideal and one of the best.

The following are ways in which one can use to control and change emotions using these concepts:

- **Self-management**

Engaging your emotional intelligence requires you to employ your emotions in making sane decisions regarding your behavior. Sometimes you may go through hard and stressful conditions such that they overpower you. At this time, you might find yourself emotionally weak thus lacking the power of managing and controlling your emotions. This may end up making you bitter and even more stressful thus might end up causing more serious problems like mental illnesses such as depression and the likes. This means that you may not be able to think or even act in a thoughtful and appropriate manner. When overwhelmed with stress, it is true that making sane and rational decisions might not be a walk in the park. At this stage, you will tend to compromise the ability to clearly organize your thoughts and even to manage your emotions, both your own and those of others in this case.

Emotions make up the most important source of information that gives you the ability to understand yourself and even tell about others around you. Apparently, in stressful situations, we get overwhelmed and might end up losing control over ourselves. With the ability to manage stress and other similar situations, we will get to stay emotionally upright and strong. This will, therefore, mean that you may receive information that tends to upset you but being emotionally strong you will not allow it to take over your emotions and thoughts. At this point, you will be able to decide and sanely make reasonable choices which will control and manage any form of impulsive behaviors or feelings. Apart from that, it is a healthy way in which you can be able to manage your emotions.

Self-management is a way in which you are able to understand your inner self thus getting to know whatever triggers your emotions, both positive and negative. By first having a full understanding of yourself, is now when you can easily relate to other people and their emotions too. At this point, it is beyond doubt that you shall be able to manage and control your emotions and even those of others at stressful circumstances that tend to provoke your emotions.

- **Social awareness**

Social awareness entails having empathy towards others in pursuit of gaining some understanding of their emotions. This enables you to easily identify and possibly interpret the cues, mainly non-verbal cues that others use when you are communicating. From these cues, you may get to understand the other person's feelings and emotional state. You can also get to understand the manner in which their emotional state changes from one moment to the other and more so whatever they term to be important. If the same non-verbal cues are used by a group of people, then that is a clear indication that these people are experiencing the same emotional crisis.

Social awareness is a concept of emotional intelligence that employs mindfulness a great deal. To be able to have strong social awareness, you might need to dig into understanding the vital importance of being mindful when socializing. This is a concept that requires you to always be present at every moment of that time as you cannot be able to identify recognize and note non-verbal cues when thinking of something else. Therefore, you should be ready to sacrifice and set aside some thoughts that might hinder your social goals. Instead, you should solemnly focus on the interaction. You should also keep track of the other person's emotions and their flow. This will ensure that you pay full attention to the manner in which your own emotions are also changing with time.

When you take time to focus on someone else's emotions, does not necessarily mean that you will be diminishing own self-awareness. In contrary to this, focusing on other people's emotions will actually aid the development of your own emotional experience and even your beliefs and values too. Therefore, through social awareness, it is very evident that you will be able to understand yourself too in the process. It is also a very good opportunity where you might get a chance of managing and possibly changing their emotions without negatively impacting them in any way. Apart from that, if you feel that something someone is talking about does not please you, then you will be learning something. From such situations is where you can be able to understand your emotions from a social perspective and thus be able to manage and possibly change them accordingly.

- **Relationship management**

Being able to identify and understand the experiences that other people go through together with emotional awareness is the basis of working with other people. With emotional awareness in place, then it means that you can perfectly now develop emotional skills which will be important to your relationship by making it more fulfilling, fruitful and effective.

Relationship management enables you to be aware of the effectiveness of how you use non-verbal cues. When communicating with others on matters linked to your feelings, it is very hard to avoid using non-verbal cues. These non-verbal cues act as stressors which loudly convey your emotions and can also aid you in reading the emotional intent of other people. Therefore, if you can recognize and understand the non-verbal cues then it means that you get the message behind it. From this, you will be able to understand one's emotions and even those of your own thus strengthening your relationship a great deal.

Relationship management also incorporates using humor as a way of relieving stress or any stressful conditions. For long humor has been regarded as the best approach to overcoming stress. This is because humor frees you from stressful thoughts that might be a burden to you and helps you to keep focus and in the right perspective. As a result of laughter, your nervous system comes into balance. You also get to be calm and stress-free thus making you be more of empathic.

In the process of being calm, you get to understand the emotions of others and most importantly your own. This will be a strong basis for managing and possibly changing emotions.

Through relationship management, you will also get to learn seeing conflicts as a great chance of growing closer to those around you. Disagreements and conflicts are very common and inevitable in human relationships. This is because two people cannot ever have the same and exact opinions, expectations or needs at all instances. This, therefore, means that conflicts and disagreeing with others are not a very bad thing but somehow normal. Being able to resolve the conflicts in a healthy and organized manner is the best approach to strengthening bonds between each one of you. This is when you can now have a chance of understanding their emotions and how they change over time. This will make it easy for you to control and change emotions easily.

- **Self-awareness**

In order to achieve fully built emotional intelligence and be able to have control and change your emotions, self-awareness is the most basic step of it all. Science of attachment usually tries to describe that a person's current emotional state is usually the result of what they have gone through earlier in life. The way in which you are capable of managing your feelings such as sadness, joy, fear, and even anger usually depends on the consistency and nature of your emotional experience earlier in life. If you were brought up by someone who cared and valued your emotions, then you would obviously grow up with your emotions being a great value to you. On the other hand, if as a young child you had confusing and painful emotions, it is much likely that you will grow up wanting to distance yourself from such emotions.

Having the ability to connect and understand your emotions and how they change from time to time is the best way to understand your emotions and how they impact your actions and thoughts. In order to build and strengthen your emotional intelligence, you need to be emotionally healthy and have the capability of reconnecting with your inner emotions and being comfortable experiencing them. This can be easily achieved by practicing mindfulness and keeping focus.

Mindfulness is the act of focusing on what is going on at the present purposefully without judging. Mindfulness helps you to avoid bad scenarios of the past that make you emotional and focus on the present while appreciating it. It, therefore, keeps you calm and makes you become focused. In this process of being calm and focused, you will be able to be more aware of yourself and more specifically your emotions.

Being self-aware and practicing mindfulness is one of the best approaches to controlling and changing your emotions. This is because you will get to understand the inner you and the circumstances which make you emotional. The act of mindfulness will allow you to forget the past that evokes emotions that might be haunting you. This will thus mean that you shall have the leeway of understanding your emotions and the way in which they keep changing from time to time. Having achieved all these, then it means that you will have control over your emotions and thus can easily change them.

Advantages of Managing Emotions Using Emotional Intelligence Concepts

Being able to control and change emotions at different circumstance accrues with various advantages in different life aspects. These advantages incorporate the end product which might be success or goal achievement. The following are some of the advantages that management and change of emotions has:

- **Achievement of set goals**

Having the ability to control and change emotions enables you to achieve the life goals that you might have set. Being able to change and control emotions enables you to focus on and embrace the present. This, therefore, means that you will forget the sad experiences of the past that may make you lose focus and in turn focus on your goals instead. This will, in turn, enable you to achieve the goals and life objectives that you might have set.

- **Keep effective communication**

If you are able to control and change your emotions, then this means that you can also understand the emotions and feelings that other people have. When communicating you will be very careful not to say what may revoke bitterness and make the other person so emotional. You will, therefore, be able to communicate with people effectively and not going to the extent of hurting their emotions and feelings.

- **Making informed decisions**

A person who is capable of controlling and changing their emotions are always focused and calm. They usually have nothing destructing them from their focus as there is no emotional interference affecting them. In this state, it means that they can calmly think about certain issues which they need to make decisions and come up with great reasonable and informed decisions.

- **Be successful**

Having the ability to control and change emotions is a calming and satisfying feeling ever. This will enable you to focus on what you are doing and avoid any distractions that might be experienced. If you are still learning, then this means that you will focus and put all your hard work into the studies. In the long run, you will notice that this will start bearing fruits and success will be on your way.

- **Embrace resilience**

Emotional management by being able to control and change emotions always makes one be hard and does not easily 'burnout'. This is because you will have the motivation to do what you like doing and not easily swayed by emotions or feelings. With time you will get focused and resilient. This means that you will be able to cope with hard situations that are very stressful at some point in life. This, therefore, proves this ability to be very vital and useful in facing the daily life activities that are usually filled with hard and challenging situations.

- **Always be happy**

People who are emotionally intelligent and can change and control their emotions usually are free from any form of stress. This is because, at situations where they feel uncomfortable with a certain emotional condition, they can easily articulate and change their emotions to favor them. In this way, they will be able to dodge all stressful situations. This will allow them to focus on situations that they feel they can handle and remain happy. If not possible to control, they can change their emotions to suit the situation and thus overcome the challenge. In this way, they will ensure that they are always happy.

Chapter 3: Strategies to Eliminate Negative Thoughts, Stress, and Fears

In this chapter, we are going to look at how to get rid of negative thoughts, stress, and fears. As we know stress, negative thoughts, and our fears can drive us into paths we never expected to end up to. We should, therefore, try as much as we can to eliminate these barriers to progress. One cannot move forward if they have negative thoughts, stress or has fears about something or someone.

Some of us are fearing things and people and we come to realize that fears are dangerous when we become old. It is, therefore, necessary to try as much as we can to get rid of our fears so that we can become of importance to ourselves and to the society at large.

Negative thoughts make us perceive almost everything negatively. Negativity can cause so much harm to a person. Someone might have planned about something and all was going on well until the person started being negative. The negative thoughts make someone live a 'don't care life'. They prevent someone from accomplishing their goals in life. Stress can make someone depressed or even get sick. We should eliminate stress, negative thoughts, and fears.

Strategies to Overcome Negative Thoughts

Always strive to find the positive side of the situation

To get rid of negative thoughts, one should always be positive despite the situation you are in. A student may be preparing for assessment tests but remembers how terribly he/she had failed in the previous tests. The student might be tempted to start having negative thoughts and says that exams do not define who we are or that maybe he/she is not gifted in academics. One should not let this happen. The student should view that as a motivation to work hard. The student should tell himself/herself that if they work hard they will be praised and admired by the teachers and staff. One should continuously work hard without giving room to negativity. Being positive about a situation helps us to overcome negative thoughts.

Do not listen to people's opinions

To overcome negative thoughts, one should not dwell much on people's thoughts and opinions. People will always have different opinions from yours and if you listen to them you will be negative about a situation. A person might say that they do not like a particular person or thing because of a particular reason and you listen to them.

Chances are you will be convinced to think as they do and this might make you be negative about something. One might want to start a car industry but then someone comes and tells you that the industry has so much difficulty, that the taxes paid are so high or that it is not a profitable business. After hearing all this, one might start thinking negatively about the car industry and even stops all plans they had in place of starting the business. One should only listen to scientifically proven facts but not mere opinions. Opinions should not be listened to if one wants to overcome negative thoughts.

Stop thinking about the thought

One should end a negative thought as soon as they realize they are being negative. One should not try to break the thought down. One should find a whole different thought about something that is not related and start thinking about it. One should not wait after hours, days or weeks so as to get rid of the thought. It should be stopped as soon as you realize it is a negative thought. If you want to stop being addicted to a drug but some time later you tell yourselves how good drugs are, that they relieve stress and they help one to relax their minds, you should stop those thoughts immediately. One may start thinking about something different like how their kids are performing at school and by that, you will have tried to eliminate negative thoughts.To eliminate negative thoughts, one should try to stop the thought and think about something else.

Talk to someone

To get rid of negative thoughts, one should find someone to talk to. There is that one person or a number of people that we always find ourselves talking to whenever we have an Issue. One who has negative thoughts should reach out to that person and talk to him/her. A problem shared is a problem half solved. When we talk to someone we feel like the burden is less. By talking to someone, we feel that there is someone who cares about us and there is someone who is always there for us. When we talk to a person about what we think, the person can help us get another dimension of thinking about the thing. Our thoughts are also made to be. One should try as much as they can not to put some thoughts into themselves. Talking to a person you trust is a great way of eliminating negative thoughts.

List down the negative thoughts

Writing down the thoughts can eliminate the thoughts. If one is thinking negatively about something, you should write it down. By writing it down, one feels like they are talking to someone. You can even picture your feelings and draw a map or a chart about something. One can even use crayons to draw what they think they are feeling. Writing helps one channel all their anger and thoughts on paper. One feels relieve d. It is similar to talking to someone but in writing, no one is listening to you. You are all by yourself and you are channeling your thoughts to the paper. Writing helps one overcome negative thoughts.

Avoid using negative terms

Negative terms should be avoided so as to eliminate negative thoughts. Negative thoughts are mostly accompanied by negative terms and negative words. Words like I am unable, I will not, It is hard, she/he also did not make it too, let it be, I am always a failure and it has never been easy among others are all terms that one should avoid. One may be used to such terms and it may seem normal saying them to oneself but one should avoid such terms. They make one not to go the extra mile. One may be saying the terms to oneself or to others. What you feed your mind is what it eats. If you tell your mind that whatever you want to do is hard, your mind will not struggle to do it since it knows it is already hard. One should get rid of words that are just negative in nature. Words like disastrous and failure should be avoided if one wants to eliminate negative thoughts. One who wants to eliminate negative thoughts should avoid the use of negative terms and words.

Talk to yourself about the thought

If you want to overcome negative thoughts, you should talk to yourself about the thought. One should hold a small meeting with oneself and try to find the cause of the thought and what he/she can do to stop thinking about it. When you get some time to yourself, you might even realize that you are just overthinking over nothing or because of a small issue that is not worth it. One can even have a special statement or word that reminds you not to be negative. One may have a statement like, 'I am a conqueror'. Whenever you are in a situation that your thoughts tell you is difficult and you say that to yourself, you always change the way you think and become positive. One can also decide to always say 'Relax you will make it' or 'Relax it is not hard'. One can decide to always include the word relax in what they say and that will always remind them to be positive when faced with a difficult situation. Use of encouraging statements can help to get rid of negative thoughts.

Understand and accept that you are thinking negatively

One who wants to get over negative thoughts should accept their thoughts. The first step is accepting who we are and what we do. Once we do that, it becomes easy for everything else. The first thing is to accept that you are thinking negatively. After accepting, you start understanding why you are thinking that way.

One should try to find the reason why you have such thoughts. One may be having negative thoughts because someone said something about the issue or because they just do not feel like it. Once you understand why you are thinking like that, you try to find a solution to your problem. If you have negative thoughts about a situation like hitting the gym because you think you might not even lose weight, ask yourself why you are thinking that way. There are people who have tremendously loosed weight due to hitting the gym and you can be among them. To eliminate negative thoughts, one should understand and accept their negative thoughts.

One can stop negative thoughts in many different ways. One can always be positive about a situation and try to find the good out of everything. One can get one of his/her confidants and tell what they are thinking and the person will help or advise accordingly. One can list his/her thoughts and get creative with what he/she is thinking. One who wants to get rid of negative thoughts should stop listening to other people's opinions and only listen to empirical-based statements and facts. One should try and talk to oneself about the thought and find out why he/she has such thoughts.

One should stop the thoughts as soon as they realize they have such thoughts. One should avoid using negative statements and words when talking to oneself and when talking to others. One should understand and accept his/her thoughts so as to stop negative thinking. There are many ways to avoid negative thoughts. These are just a few which negative thinkers should try to implement.

Strategies to Eliminate Stress

Identify the root of the stress

Finding the cause of why you are stressed is an important step that can help to eliminate stress. There are times when one feels stresses or one feels uncomfortable and thinks a lot about something yet the person is not sure what the issue is. To get rid of stress, one should find what is causing you to be stressed up. One should commit some 'lone time' and talk to oneself and find out why they are stressed out. To find what makes you stressed, you should ask yourself questions like; who is concerned in this? Why did I do yesterday? Who was I with when this happened? Such questions help one identify the cause of the stress easily. Identifying what causes stress is the first step to eliminating stress.

Get rid of commitments that are not necessary

One should avoid getting committed to things that are not necessary. Depending on who you are and what you do, we all have different commitments. One may be committed to their children, their marriage partner, their work, their education, their spiritual knowledge and much more. It is for a person to know what commitments are necessary and which are not. One should only concentrate on things that are important to them. You might find a person putting so much effort into something that should be done by another person. You should let everyone play their role. It is through having all those commitments that are not necessary for your thoughts, that you find yourself stressed. The moment one gets rid of unnecessary commitments, one becomes focused and does not get stressed up. One should only be committed to necessary things only.

Avoid postponing

Postponing should be avoided if one wants to get rid of stress. At times we say we will do things at a later time or at a later date mostly because we are lazy or because we have something else we are doing at the moment. Procrastination is the thief of time. One should do tasks and things immediately as they emerge to avoid having so many things to do at a particular time. When one postpones, you come to realize later that you have no time left and you have loads of work to do. This makes one stressed out thinking of how they will manage to be done perfectly and on time. A simpler solution to all this is to do things the scheduled time. By this, you will always meet the timeline and will not be stressed out. One who wants to get rid of stress should do things the scheduled time and avoid postponing.

Be organized

One should do things in an organized manner and in a neat way to avoid stress. At times we might plan things and everything falls into place but there is that one time that we slide and try to squeeze in something. This squeezing in may make us stressed up as there is no place for what we have squeezed in. Disorganization may also stress out someone when you urgently need something but you cannot find it because you are not sure where it is. One might be looking for a certain certificate that is needed for a job interview and it is urgent but you do not find it because you are disorganized. This will make you lose the chance to get the job and in turn, you become stressed. If the person was organized they would have known the certificate is in a certain drawer or bag and they get it out and they get a chance to get the job. One who wants to avoid stress should not be disorganized but should plan everything in an organized manner.

Do not be late

One who wants to be stress-free should always do things on time. When one is behind his/her schedule, one tends to be stressed up. We should try as much as we can to be punctual enough so as to start things on time and finish on time. When one is late when doing something, you always feel stressed up. When you have an exam at 8 and you are not in the exam room by 8 you get stressed. One thinks of the many possibilities that could happen if one missed the chance. If you are late you will have to redo the exam. This will make you stressed and you will start blaming yourself for not being punctual enough. If you are late to go to the bus station and the bus leaves before you are there you will have to get other means of traveling, this makes you stressed up while searching for another means of transport. One should try as much as possible to always be punctual and do things at the right time.

Do not control others or things

If you do not want to get stressed out, do not control things or other people. We do not have the power to do that and whenever we force ourselves to do that, we get stressed because things might not really turn out as we expect. One might think that if you control a person and tell them to do a certain job for you will make it easier for you. The person may or may not do the job, whatever they do is under their control not under your control. If they decide not to do what you had told them, you will have to do the job. Doing the job means you will have to fix that at a particular time which means you will have to do it in a hurry. You can only give directions and controls to yourself. A person of sound mind will do what they want regardless of whether it is right or wrong. You should just let things flow as planned but not as you wish. You should respect other people's decisions and the way they control their things. One who wants to avoid stress does not control other people but only controls himself/herself.

Avoid people who stress you out

To avoid stress, one should avoid people who stress him/her. There are people who when we meet we just feel stressed out. They can be our employers, teachers, parents, colleagues, relatives or even friends. One should avoid being in the presence of such people because they will always stress you out. If your employer stresses you out, try to avoid him/her. It can be that whenever your employer sees you in the wrong they remind you of a past event that stresses you out. An employer might see you trying to fix live wires and they start mocking you saying how the last time you tried doing that the firm lost a lot of property in a fire. Maybe whenever you remember that incident you get stressed out. One should avoid such people as they will only do you more harm than good. One who wants to avoid stress should avoid people that cause them to be stressed.

Appreciate everything and everyone in life

If you want to avoid stress, always appreciate everyone and everything life gives you. One should learn to show gratitude. Sometimes we stress up because things did not end up as we expected. Maybe you were doing an exam and you get a grade B while you were expecting to get an A. You should appreciate whatever life offers you. When life gives you lemons, make a cocktail out of it. Do not ask for more. That is what you got and that is what is yours. You will not get another so you should just accept and strive to do better the next time. If you want to be associated with a particular group of people because you think they are cool but you end up being in another group of people, appreciate them. You can still be happy with them if not happier. When we learn to appreciate what we have, we will not get stressed up.

Exercise and eat foods that are healthy

If you want to reduce stress, eat healthy foods and do a lot of exercises. Exercise rejuvenates our body and makes us stronger. When you exercise your mood changes and you become happy. Exercise and eating healthy go hand in hand. There are foods that make one moody and there are foods that do not have mood effects on a person. A healthy person is less prone to stress. Exercise does not leave room for stress in a person's body. Exercise also gives one some time for himself/herself. As you exercise, you think more about yourself and the situations you are in. This prevents one from getting stressed as they have a plan of their lives. Eating healthily and doing exercise regularly can help reduce stress.

Plan to do important things only

If you want to avoid stress, have a to-do-list of important things only. One should not put loads of works on their list. There are things that even if you do they will not impact on you. One should get rid of such activities. Concentrate on things and activities that are important and necessary. If you think something does not help you in any way get rid of it. One who keeps a long to-do-list without caring whether it is helpful or not is prone to be stressed. This is because the person has each 0f their minute planned on and whenever they try to fix some time for themselves in between they will mess things up. One should only strive to do things that are important to you and leave out other things. To avoid stress, one should create a to-do-list of important activities only.

Do what you like most

One who wants to reduce stress levels or get rid of it completely should practice doing what they like doing most. We are all different and we have different preferences. Our talents, hobbies, and abilities are different. Different people may like doing different things like listening to music, taking a walk, going to the movies, skating, playing tennis, helping others, playing soccer, reading novels and books or even writing blogs. One should put so much attention to what they like. The body wants what it wants. If you give the body what it wants, you will not become stressed up easily. People find their happiness from small things. I personally listen to music find myself in a fantasy world. When you do what you like doing, you will spend most of your time being happy. One who wants to get rid of stress should spend their free time doing activities that they find fun doing.

Talk to someone

One who is stressed should find someone to talk to. The person can be a friend. A relative or anyone you trust. When you talk to someone you feel better. It is through talking to someone that you get to exchange thoughts. When you talk to someone the person gives his/her ideas and thoughts on a particular issue. The thoughts of the person can help you get a new perspective to a new thing. When you talk to someone you feel you have gotten something off your chest. It is important to talk to someone when stressed out.

Talking to another person when stressed prevents depression. To avoid stress one should reach out and talk to someone about the issue at hand.

Be assertive

One who wants to eliminate stress should always mean what they say. When one says yes, they should mean their yes and when they say no they should mean their no. One should not be influenced by others to do things or not to do things. You might do things because you were influenced by someone then when the consequences come to be you regret alone and be stressed out. Everything has its own consequences. One should, therefore, make assertive decisions after critical thinking. One should not do something because his/her friends have done it but should do what is right. The right thing is usually hard to do but we should strive to do it. The simpler thing is mostly the wrong thing. Wrong things have negative consequences which will get you stressed. To avoid stress, one should mean and do what they say.

Take caffeine in regular amounts

Caffeine should be taken in the correct amounts by someone who wants to get rid of stress. Caffeine is a stimulant. It is found in a drink like tea and coffee. One should take such drinks in regular amounts as they contain caffeine which increases anxiety levels. People are different and each person has a maximum caffeine intake. One should try not to exceed it as it will increase anxiety and stress levels.

Stress should be avoided and in case one gets to be stressed they should try to eliminate it. There are many ways in which one can avoid stress. One should avoid situations and people that make him/her stressed. One should avoid commitments that are not necessary. One should not postpone things and do things at the scheduled time. One should always be organized and never be late to do anything. One should not give himself/herself the mandate to control another person or thing. One should have a simple to-do-list that is made up of important things only. One who wants to get rid of stress should exercise and eat healthy foods. One should use their free time to do what they like doing most. One should have a regular caffeine intake depending on their threshold. One should practice gratitude and appreciate others and whatever they get to have in life. One should always be assertive and strive to do the right thing always. One should talk to someone if they feel stressed out. There are many ways of eliminating stress. Above are just a few.

Strategies to Eliminate Our Fears

Know what your fears are

One who wants to eliminate their fears should start knowing what his/her fears are. We all have different fears. Each person has his/her own fear. One can fear height, water, darkness, spiders, being alone or flying just to name a few. When one realizes that they fear a particular thing or person, they should accept that they fear those things. After one has accepted, they should not try to hide from them. If you fear something, you should realize that it will never end. If you fear darkness, there is no time that will come for darkness to cease to exist. Knowledge is power. When you have the knowledge of your fears, you will not find yourself in hard situations when faced with your fears. Knowing your fears should be the first step taken by one who wants to get rid of their fears.

Learn to appreciate

One who wants to overcome fear should learn how to show gratitude. When you learn to be appreciative of things you have and situations you are in, you will get rid of fear. If you fear flying on a plane, be appreciative that you got the chance to fly in a plane. If you fear to lose a job, appreciate that you currently are doing the job and you have not lost the job. When you learn to show gratitude when faced with your fears, you will view the positive side of you will have fewer emotions connected to the fear. When you show gratitude to someone or something, one feels good. It is good to appreciate something if it is nice. One who wants to eliminate stress should practice the act of gratitude.

Discover what emotions are associated with fear

One who wants to eliminate fear should identify the feeling or emotion connected to the fear they have. One might have different feelings or thoughts for different fears. You might feel shocked when you see a spider, you might feel anxious when flying on a plane and you do not know when you will get down, you might feel sad when you think of losing your job and when you think of everything that will happen when you lose the job. Mostly when someone thinks of their fear they start to overthink and they get different emotions while thinking. You might be having the fear of failing an exam and when you think about it you feel pitiful for yourself, then you remember how much your parents have struggled to see you in school you start hating yourself and much more feelings. These are the reasons why one should identify the emotions and feelings they get when they face their fears.

List them down

One who wants to get over their fears will list them down. Most times thinking about our fears only gets us stressed. At times it makes us even more stressed than we were before. It is therefore wise for someone to list their fears down if they want to get rid of them. When you list them down, you feel better and you feel relieved just a little bit. Writing helps us to express what is in our thoughts and what we feel. When writing, one should not be restricted to a particular concern but should list all that is in their mind. One can even go further and start drawing what they think they feel or have in their chest when they are associated with that fear. One who wants to get rid of their fears should write them down.

Talk to someone

Talking to someone about your fears will help you eliminate your fears. One might have had a fear of flying and they decide to talk to someone. When talking to the person about your fear, they tell you that they have flown several times and it is fun and maybe you should try it out with them. This might help you get a better image of flying. When you talk to a person about your fears and what you feel about your fears, the person tries as much as they can to change the situation. One might not necessarily change your perception towards your fear but they might help you know how to face it. They might give you stories or testimonies of people who have made it through and you encourage yourself and hope all will be well. One should make sure that after talking to a person they should not leave the person the way they came in terms of facing and handling the fear. Talking to someone can be a great way of eliminating our fears.

Learn not to control things

To eliminate fear, one should not control situations or things. A person might think that because they are good at something they can never fail or make a slight mistake at it. We are humans and we can never be perfect. You might be a punctual employee always on doing your tasks and obedient but one day you might delay a bit and you will get your fear from that. You will not know how to face your employer because you have always told yourself you are the best and no one can beat you at being punctual. You start fearing that the employer might fire you or you start fearing that the employer might but you down there in the hierarchy. We should not control things or people if we want to get rid of our fears.

Learn from others

One who wants to get rid of their fear should learn from others. There are many people who share a common fear. Some have managed to get through it while some are struggling to get over it. One who wants to eliminate their fears should reach out to such people. If someone already made it overcome the fear, find out what they did to overcome the fear. If you find people who are still struggling to get over it, learn what they are doing. Every day should be a learning day to someone who wants to get rid of their fears. You should even try to associate yourselves with people who have the same fear as you have and are trying to overcome it. One may fear to break up with a spouse and when you go to your friends who have the same issue, they tell you what they do to always see they are together. To eliminate your fears, you should learn from other people who have or who had the same fear as you.

Pray or meditate

One who wants to get rid of their fears should pray and ask for help. Christians are taught that God listens and answers our prayers. There are times you struggle with something so much that you do not know what to do next. One who has reached this stage should try and seek help from a religious perspective. Christians should ask God for help and Muslims should ask Allah to answer their prayers. This depends on the religious background of a person. I am a Christian and I personally believe that whatever you ask shall be given unto you. If one is not religious or finds it hard to pray, one can meditate. Meditation is as good as praying and helps one to overcome their fears too. One should choose whatever they think will be effective for them. A person who wants to get rid of his/her fears should pray or meditate.

Accept that everyone makes mistakes

One who wants to get rid of his/her fears should understand that no one is perfect and we all make mistakes. Some of our fears are caused by failing. One might have the fear of failing a test, of not doing well at the place of work, of not emerging the best in a fashion show or of not meeting the sales of a particular item. We should, however, understand that we have all experienced points in our lives when we failed at a particular thing. One cannot always be successful at everything you do and if that happens you are not doing something right. One should, therefore, understand that failure opens a road for success. When you fail chances are people will mock or laugh at you while others will hold your hand and show you the way. It is therefore up to us to decide what we emerge out as after failure. We should not be defined by failure. One who wants to get rid of fear should not let failure put them down.

Let life be

One who wants to get rid 0f his/her fears should flow with the events of life. If you want to live life peacefully, just flow with the way things are. At times we create fears because of people's opinions about us and how they judge us. One fears to talk in front of a large crowd because you are afraid of the impression you have on people or because you are afraid that people will talk about you. One should not let their fears be based on such small issues. People will always speak their views and thoughts about something or someone and because we all have different preferences we should not let that bother us. Maybe when you do something great some people will not notice because they are not destined for greatness. After all, people have talked about you severally and life went on after that. Even with our fears, we should just flow with life in case we face them. One might be at 45 years and have a fear of losing his/her job and they eventually lose it. Being 45 years that might not be the first job you have lost. After losing the first job life continued as usual. We do not know what life holds for each one of us. One who wants to get rid of his/her fear should just let life be and flow with everything as it happens.

There are many strategies one can use to eliminate his/her fears. One should start with identifying his/her fear and dig to know what emotions and feelings are associated with fear. Once one has known what emotions are connected with the fear, they should find a way to control the emotion or feeling. One should talk to someone about their fears or talk to trained personnel and if they find that hard they can write their thoughts about the fear down. One should seek religious help by praying and if they find that hard they can meditate. One should understand that failure is not permanent and everyone at some point has failed in a particular thing. One should not create fears because they are afraid of peoples' opinions and thoughts. One should flow with life because even after everything happens life will go on. One should learn to appreciate the opportunities they have and not view them as fears.

Negative thoughts, stress, and fears are all things that can cause us to be mentally ill and depressed. They are concerned with our cognitive behavior and one should try to eliminate them as soon as they realize they have developed them. They can be hard to avoid and eliminate but one should try as much as they can to get rid of them. There are strategies that apply to all three issues. Strategies, like talking to someone, writing them down, exercising and eating healthy and praying or meditating, can all help eliminate the issues. One who wants to eliminate negative thinking, stress or his/her fears should struggle as much as they can since it is not easy. There are times when one gets halfway there and loses hope because they cannot see the fruits their efforts but that should not be a reason for them to stop. One who has made a personal decision to eliminate all these do not turn back.

Chapter 4: Strategies of Anger Management to Reach Calmness and Build-Up Self Control

It is normal to have anger issues. It is an emotion that is normal and it is not bad or good. When we get angry, we are communicating that we are not happy about the things people have told us. It is just a way of telling people around us that we were not happy about their actions. Anger can also be said to be a way that one uses to communicate their frustrations or even issues that may be threatening their peace.

There are those times when one finds themselves just angry for no reason.

When it becomes extreme, it can cost people relationships and also make them psychologically disturbed which may make them lose focus and also deprive them of a good quality of life. There are people who do not show anger and so they will pile it up. Piling up anger may have very negative effects on one's well-being. They may have long term negative impact which becomes difficult when not controlled.

Anger is something that can be managed with proper control. It is important for people to understand that anger is not bad when it is under control. It becomes bad when it makes people behave in a way that can make the people around them uncomfortable. It also becomes an issue when people harm themselves as a result of anger.

People will get angry when they see someone abusing children when they are mental or emotionally abused and also when they find themselves in traumatic situations. They may also become angry when they lack sleep when they have low self-esteem and also when they are stressed and anxious. It is important to ensure that you look for help early enough in order to avoid anger at all costs.

One is required to ensure that they find a solution to this problem early enough in order for them to ensure that they remain calm and for them to avoid anger. When one wants to manage anger, they do not need to hold it inside them. They should talk about it and take measures to ensure that they are free from it. For one to be able to manage their anger, they should be able to accept that they actually have anger issues. When one finds out that their anger issues are making them lose control, they would need to look for help.

There are those signs that will stand out when one has anger issues. However, there are those extreme cases which will tell you that you need help from a professional. I have listed some of the signs that one will experience and make a decision to look for professional help.

1. When they find themselves on the wrong side of the law
2. When they find themselves suppressing their anger all the time

3. Having fights with people around them and also their family from time to time
4. When they find themselves confronting people around them because of petty issues
5. Becoming violent towards people an even threatening them
6. When they find themselves breaking things in the house when they get angry
7. When they lose their temper over small issues

When you find yourself in any of the above cases, then you need help. It is at this point that one might need help with managing their anger since it will be evident that the anger is having some negative influence on them. It will also be having some negative impact on the people around which may make them judge you wrongly. It is also said that anger can have some effects on one's health as well as causing them to have an issue with people around them.

When one has anger issues, they may get heart diseases and insomnia as well as finding themselves with high blood pressure. It may also hinder your concentration which may make you feel frustrated since you may not be able to handle all the things around you with ease. This will also make it hard for you to enjoy life since you will not have an easy time interacting with people.

Whenever people find themselves struggling with anger, they should look for help from counselors. This will enable them to live a life that is free from stress. You will also be able to relate well with your friends, colleagues, and employers without experiencing any challenges. For one to be able to control their anger, they should follow the following steps:

- Being able to recognize signs of anger early enough
- Giving yourself time to think about it and identify the triggers
- Using strategies that will be of help in control of anger

There are many things that one can apply in life in order for them to be able to manage their anger. I have discussed some of them below.

Find Out Reasons for your Anger

Am sure most of you have gotten into a fight because of some things that would be considered petty. After thinking through the things that made you fight, you may have discovered that it was something that you could actually have solved without an issue. For someone to make sure that they are in control of their anger, they have to ensure that they find its real cause.

When you know the cause of your anger, you will be able to use the means possible to eliminate it. You will also be able to look for strategies which would help you to be able to overcome your frustrations which will help you to deal with the anger issues as they arise. Frustrations will mostly come as a result of not being understood or when one is not understanding the people around them. it would be important to identify the things that make you angry and ensure that you get away from them. This will help a lot in avoiding anger.

When you find out the reasons for your anger, you will also be able to keep away from the things that make you angry. There are people who may have anger issues as a result of growing up a place that they were not given a chance to express how they feel. This means that they could stomach all kinds of mistreatments without saying a word. As a result of their frustrations, they become so sensitive to the things said to them. A very minor thing can accelerate their anger to a level that all the people around them cannot even understand.

When you have grown up in an area that does not allow you to express your feelings, you will always find yourself using anger to solve issues. This is because you were only trained to bottle up feelings. It would be advisable to seek counseling in order for you to learn some strategies that you can apply when something angers you. Counselors are skilled and knowledgeable about the things that may be of help to you when it comes to handling anger issues.

It is very easy to manage anger when you know its cause. You can even learn how to control it by yourself. This is because there is a lot of information about it on the internet which I will be helpful to you. This means that a person who has accepted that they have anger issues can look for information that can help them overcome it from anywhere.

Acting on Anger Signs Early Enough

You may find yourself just exploding as a result of anger without any warning. Even before you get angry, you feel it in yourself some emotions which could be making you feel uncomfortable about various situations. Those are the signs that you need to be aware of since they are the ones that make you feel angry. Being aware of such emotions is very important since one will be able to get away from the people who may be making them angry. They are also able to control their anger when faced with situations that require them to control themselves.

By doing this, one will be able to control their anger before it comes out since the anger may affect people around them. One is required to listen to their body and when they are angry and convince their mind that it isn't right to get angry over issues. They can choose to walk away which will be of help to them since they will be able to avoid getting angry.

When people with anger issues feel the signs of anger, they should be able to choose not to get angry. They can even choose to see the good sign of the situation that is making them angry. By doing this they will be able to live a positive life that is free from anger. They will also be able to have good relationships with people around them which will make them relate well with them without any conflicts.

Identifying your Triggers

It is important for one to identify the things that make them angry. They may be getting easily irritable because of stressful situations. The stressful situations do not mean that one must get angry, they should be able to take control of their anger even when they are under pressure. One can check on their day to day activities and identify those activities that trigger anger in them. By doing this, they can choose to change the routine and come up with one that is not too stressful for them. They can also choose to avoid those activities and replace them with a positive thing or something that they love doing.

One may be going out with a group of people and the end results become fights and abuses which make them angry. They can avoid going out with such people as it will help them to be able to avoid getting angry. It is important for one to ensure that they get rid of the bad company since they will make sure that their anger levels are controlled and they may also avoid getting triggered into getting angry.

People may think that their anger comes from internal sources but the truth is that they may come from your interpretation of the issues you may be facing. Someone may be giving out ideas that may change a situation but someone with anger issues will interpret them depending on their mood about it. They may be triggering their anger through overgeneralizing issues and also through jumping into conclusions about them.

Triggers may also come from blaming people for your misfortunes and also your failures. It is therefore important for people to be able to discover the things that trigger anger in them in order for them to be able to avoid getting angry. By doing so, they will be able to have a good relationship with the people around them.

Identify Ways of Cooling Down Quickly

When one is trying to manage their anger, they should be able to look for ways to ensure that they cool down when anger issues arise. They should be able to tell that they are about to get angry through the triggers. By identifying that, they will be able to avoid things that make them angry in order for them to feel better about themselves. There are many strategies that one can apply in order for them to be able to cool down easily after an argument. I have listed them below.

Taking Some Deep Breath: When one gets some anger triggers, they should be able to calm down, take a deep breath in order for them to release any tension within them. The deep breath will help them to relax and feel better about the situation that they may be going through. They will also be able to avoid feeling angry which will be of great help to them.

Focussing on Other Things: When one feels angry, they can try to focus on other things that are not related to the situation that they may be facing. Focussing on those things will make them forget the issues that are making them angry. They may also find other positive things that may make them keep going. They may also get some distractions which will make them cool down and even forget about the issues that may be making them angry.

Taking a Walk: When one feels angry, taking a walk will be of great help in lowering their anger levels. As they walk, they will get some distractions along the way which will make them forget that there were things that were making them angry. They may meet friends along the way and may end up catching up on various things. This helps a lot in lowering their levels of anger. Walking helpful in so many ways. It helps people to be able to freshen up and release all the tension within them. They are also able to look at nature and appreciate it. They will feel peaceful since by the time they get back they will have cooled down.

Engaging in Physical Activities: There are people who join the gym or do some physical activities at home. The activities are very important in helping one to cool down when they are angry. This is because one releases a lot of tension when doing them. People who may have gone there when angry will leave the place having cooled down as a result of the activities they will have carried out in the gym.

As they carry out different activities, they get distracted from the challenges that they may be experiencing which make them forget that they were angry. It is therefore important for one to take part in physical activities in order for them to be able to cool down when they suspect that they are going to get angry.

Whenever one is feeling angry they need to ask themselves some questions like whether it is really worth it to get angry about a given issue. They should also ask themselves if the issue making them angry is really worth ruining their day. They can also ask themselves if there is something they can do about the issue that may be making them angry and also whether taking any action will be worth their time.

By asking yourself those questions, one will be able to decide whether to get angry about the situation or not. In case any of the issues making them angry needs them to act on them, one will be able to act on them without regretting the consequences of the outcome. People around you will also understand you when you get angry because the issue that may have made you angry will be genuine unlike when you get angry because of small issues.

Find Healthy Ways of Expressing Anger

When one gets angry for a situation that is worth getting angry about, they should ensure that they look for mature solutions to the problems they may be facing. They need to ensure that however severe the situation is, they come up with ways of solving the issues without complicating the issue more. They should come up with ways of ensuring that they deal with the issues in a healthy manner which ensures that nobody comes out of it hurt. When one comes up with better ways of solving issues, they maintain good relationships with the people around them. They are able to interact with people around them easily without conflicting or experiencing any challenges.

People who were one quick to anger are able to build healthy relationships with people when they learn ways of dealing with their anger. People will start relating well with them because they will see that they are changed and that they are able to control their anger. It is therefore important to ensure that one finds of dealing with their anger issues in order for them to build healthier relationships with people.

People who are determined to make their relationship work should ensure that they work on making the relationships stronger rather than being the winner in the relationship. This will help them to gain trust with the people around them and also respect is automatically cultivated amongst themselves.

When people are arguing, it is important to ensure that they do not focus on the disagreements they had in the past. They should focus on just the current issues in order for them to avoid complicated issues. When you focus on the issues that may be making you angry now, you will be able to ensure that you solve the issue without experiencing any challenges.

One needs to also ensure that they have the willingness to forgive those who make them angry. They should learn that forgiveness is the only thing that can lessen the burden in their heart. It is easier to deal with issues when you do not have a grudge with anyone. When you have a burden in your heart, you make easily irritable. This is because you still have some underlying issues. It is important to ensure that you handle all the issues as they come in order for you to avoid pilling up issues with people in your heart.

It is also important to ensure that you know the right time to let go. Whenever you find yourself in a disagreement, you should be able to tell when it is the right time to stop it. Whenever you find out that you cannot disagree on anything, you would need to end the argument by taking the burden. In this case, no one will win or lose the argument. This will make things neutral and will leave everybody in peace.

Staying Calm by Taking Care of Yourself

When one decides to take care of themselves, they are likely to achieve overall mental, physical and emotional health. They will remain peaceful since they know and understand the things that make them angry and those that don't. They are able to manage their stress well which enables them to be in control of the issues that stress them and avoid them completely.

When one is calm, they are able to think through all the issues before acting on them. If they figure out that reacting to some issues will not benefit them in any way, they should avoid getting angry because of them. This will help a lot in ensuring that you stay calm and avoid trouble. There are those people who will only be able to stay calm by they talk to a trusted friend. They have to open up to someone in order for them to remain calm. If you are that type of person, ensure that you open up to someone that you can trust.

There are people who will spread the things you share with them with other people. This will only complicate things more. The trust you had for them will break as a result of that. Lastly, ensure that you get enough sleep. When you have enough sleep, you will be able to eliminate any negative thoughts that you may be having. You will also have enough rest which will help in improving your focus on other things so you won't have time to get involved in issues that will make you angry.

Using Humour to Relieve Tension

When things get tough, it is important to apply humor in order to lighten people's mood. Humour makes people forget the challenges they are facing for a moment. One can also use humor when they want to pass sensitive information. Humour will help a lot in ensuring that people who are likely to get mad at you do not get mad. This enables you to be able to communicate your point without making people angry.

It is important to note that you are supposed to laugh with them and not laugh at them. By doing this, you will be able to ensure that they are all comfortable with the joke. Humour is, therefore, able to reduce stress, lower tension levels and also lower one's anger. This helps a great deal in ensuring that you avoid conflicts with people around you. This gives people a good environment to work and relax.

Know When You Need Professional Help

You may be able to put all the measures to ensure that you manage your anger but you may still need professional help. You should be in a position to tell that you have done your best but you still need professional help. There are people who try their best to ensure that they control their anger but they hit their dead-end on this. It is at this time that they will need to look for a professional counselor who will help them to be able to manage their anger.

When you decide to look for professional help, it will help you a great deal. This is because you will be able to meet other people battling anger which will give you the motivation to know that you are not battling anger issues alone. It will motivate you to work on your anger in order for you to be able to achieve better results. When there, you will be able to get therapies and counseling which will help you to be able to achieve your goal. Seeing a professional is therefore very important in ensuring that you finally manage to handle your anger issues.

Make sure that you Think Before you speak

Many are times when you find yourself overreacting to issues because of not thinking them through before you speak. You will find yourself regretting because of speaking about the issue when you are still angry. It is important to ensure that when you feel angry, you take your time to collect your thoughts before you speak. By doing this, you will be able to only speak about the things that make sense. You will also be able to control your anger which will help in making sure that you are reasonable enough.

There are those times when you will find yourself arguing with someone who is not reasonable. This will make you angrier. The best thing to do is to give the person time to calm down. Once they calm down, you will be able to discuss the issue with them which will help in ensuring that you achieve the best results.

Therapy

Therapy is one of the things that have been used by people in order for them to be able to control their anger. They may attend the therapy sessions as individuals or as groups. Through the sessions, they are able to get help in the identification of triggers that may be making them angry. They also get to learn the ways of handling the triggers and making sure that they do not cause anger in you. Therapists also teach people techniques to apply in order for them to overcome anger. They ensure that they see things positively which enables them to solve problems without experiencing any challenges.

Keeping an Anger Diary

An anger diary is a record that people keep for them to be able to follow up on their anger patterns. They can list all the things that made them angry that day and the reasons why they got angry. This helps them a lot in ensuring that they are able to anticipate when triggers are likely to happen. Once they predict them, they will be able to cope with them effectively which helps them to cope with anger.

When writing down the information, they can also note down the strategies that worked and those that did not work. This will help them to be able to apply those that they are sure they will work and get rid of those did not work. By doing all this, they will be able to control their anger which will help them to lead a better healthier life.

Through the diary, one can also write down the positive things that happened to them during the day. This will be of great help in ensuring that one sees that apart from the negative things, there were also positive things that happened to them. This will act as a motivation to achieve more positive things each day than the negative ones.

It is very important for people to have self-control if at all they want to be able to manage their anger. One will have to ensure that they are consistent with what they choose to have some self-control in order for them to eliminate anger in their lives.

They may be required to practice some of the things that I have listed below in order for them to be able to control their anger.

- **Having a Positive Attitude**

When one has a positive attitude, it becomes very easy for them to handle issues. This is because they believe that they can do it and they put all the necessary measures to ensure that they achieve all the set goals. It also feels great when one is in control of their situations. It motivates them to do even better since they are determined to conquer everything. With a positive attitude, it is likely that you will not feel angry about the issues that are meant to annoy you. This is because you will look at the bright side of it and be able to face it and solve it successfully.

- **Setting Goals**

It is important for people to set goals if they want to be in control of the issues facing them. They need to come up with rules to follow when people or situations make them angry. They are then expected to follow those rules to the latter. They have to ensure that they are disciplined enough to deal with the issues without breaking the rules. This will help them to be able to control their anger since they have no room for making mistakes.

By achieving those goals, they will have made a step ahead which will ensure that they are self-controlled. Achieving the goals makes them motivated since. They will even go an extra mile in order to ensure that they achieve the goals. They should also ensure that they set achievable goals. They can even start with short term goals before they set long term goals. Once the short term ones, they will be able to slowly add the goals in order for them to be able to be consistent which in return will enable them to achieve the goals.

- **Self-Monitoring**

One will be able to tell whether they are achieving the set goals through monitoring the progress they are making in all the areas. Self-monitoring gives them feedback on their progress. When you monitor yourself, you will ensure that you are following all the rules that you are required to follow. You will make sure that all the goals are achieved within the given timelines. By doing this, you will be able to control your anger issues and with time, you will be free from anger.

Self-monitoring is also said to help one to avoid losing track of the goals they have set. They will make sure that they are following all the rules in order to ensure that they lower their anger issues. Once they succeed in this, they will note that their anger levels will have gone lower by great levels.

- **Through motivation**

Motivation works so well, especially with children. They can be given presents for not getting angry for a given period of time. They get motivated to achieve the goal within the set period. Motivation also works for adults. The may get rewarded for controlling their anger. The rewards make them strive to be able to achieve their goals which enables them to also feel better about themselves.

People will mostly stick to something as a result of the value they get from it. No one will stick to something that is not benefiting them in any way. One gets motivated through their achievements so little or no achievements makes them less motivated. People need to, therefore, ensure that they set goals that they can achieve in order for them to get the motivation to control their anger and to also work on the things that may be making them angry.

- **Confidence**

Confidence is so important in so many areas of our lives. When one has confidence that they will achieve a certain goal, they will definitely achieve the goals. When they decide that they will work on their anger issues, they will achieve that since they have the confidence required to achieve it. They will, therefore, take up the issue and work on it and believe that they will lower their anger issues. It is therefore important to ensure that one gathers confidence to say no to anger and by doing so, they will be able to get rid of the burden of anger.

- **Have the Willpower**

Willpower is referred to as having the strength and also psychological energy which one needs in order for them to be able to set goals and achieve them. It's also having the strength to overcome any kinds of temptations which will enable them to be able to achieve all the goals that they have set. Having willpower is very important as it helps one to keep moving even after the going gets tough. They do not give up since they are only focussed on the goal.

Through willpower, they are also able to have some self-control which helps them to control their anger even when they are tempted to feel angry. When one is able to control themselves, they get rid of anger little by little. This means that they are able to achieve their goal with the set time.

- **Monitor their pattern of behavior**

It is important for people with anger issues to ensure that they monitor their pattern of behavior. This will help them to tell the things that make them angry and those that do not. They should be able to get rid of the behaviors that make them angry even as they try to work on their anger. Monitoring your pattern is crucial since it enables you to ensure that you maintain discipline which will in return help you to get rid of anger issues.

Monitoring your pattern of behavior will also ensure that you do not repeat the mistakes that you did in the past. This is because you will be able to apply self-control whenever the issues arise which will help you avoid getting angry. It is also through monitoring your behavior patterns that you will be able to avoid situations that make you angry and also be able to remain calm even when you are provoked by the people around you.

There are very many reasons why people chose to control their anger. One of the reasons being the benefits that come with it. Below are some of the benefits that one gets from being able to control their anger.

Being Able to Deal with Issues Soberly

When one overcomes their anger, they are able to deal with the issues that arise in a sober manner. This means that they do not have conflicts with the people around them since you will be in control of your emotions and also feelings. One is also able to have meaningful relationships since there will be no fights between them. Whenever any of them is angry, they will be able to talk about it and solve the issues without getting angry. They will be able to agree that there is a problem and deal with it without experiencing any kind of conflict.

One Becomes more Empathetic

When one is in control of their anger, they are able to have empathy for others. This is because they are more understanding and reasonable. Whenever they get angry, they are able to get away from it without experiencing any challenges.

It is very important for people to ensure that they deal with their anger issues. This will enable them to be able to look at issues in a positive manner. By doing this, they will be able to see issues in other peoples perspective which will help them to understand them.

Doing this will help people to understand each other and build better relationships amongst themselves.

One Gains New Insights

When one decides to deal with their anger issues, they get to learn from their mistakes. As they go through the healing process, they are able to see where they went wrong which helps them to work on the issue. They are also able to be in control of all the issues they are going through since they are now fully aware of the issues. They are able to treat people better, cooperate with them which in the ends enables them to build healthy connections with people.

They are Less Stressed

When people are angry, they are likely to be stressed throughout that period. This is because they do not have peace within themselves so they will tend to quarrel, everyone, they interact with. Many are times which they will be involved in confrontations as a result of piled up issues. Once they deal with the anger issues, they are able to calm down, make peace with other people and also relate well with them. By doing this, they are able to make better friends and maintain them since they are in control of their feelings. This makes them have some peace of mind which helps them to live well with the people around them.

One Becomes Less Aggressive and More Assertive

When one is angry, they become unreasonable. This is because they are selfish and think that they are the only ones being made angry. What they don't know is that the situations making them angry can be avoided. They can communicate well which would help them in understanding each other better. They need to be assertive when it comes to communication in order for them to be able to have a clear channel of communication which they can use. Through it, they will be able to become less aggressive and more aggressive.

One Becomes Responsible for their Actions

It is important for one to know that they are the only ones who are responsible for their actions when angry. Everything they do should be thought through in order to ensure that you do not regret your actions later. This means that when one manages their anger, they are able to identify issues that may annoy them and be able to avoid them. It also means that they have learned to keep all annoying situations in control which makes them calm down when they are angry. Being responsible for your actions is therefore very important as it helps one to be cautious when dealing with issues.

One Gets to Build Better Relationships

When one has anger issues, they tend to push the people they love away. They may avoid holding conversations with them since they feel angry at everybody around them. Most of them will do this when they realize that they are hurting them. There are others who will keep away from their loved ones when they make them angry. One, therefore, makes good relationships with them as a result of controlling their anger. They will bring them closer and ensure that they do not hurt them again.

It is therefore important for people to ensure that they work on their anger issues early enough in order to ensure that they do not spread the anger to the people around them. By doing this, they will not only have helped themselves but also the people they engage in their day to day lives. Whenever they are not able to handle the anger themselves, they should look for help from professionals who are experienced in this area. At the end of it all, they will be able to live a happy life which is free from anger.

Chapter 5: How to Use Your Emotions for Personal Growth and to Improve Relationships

To manage our anger, as we have seen in chapter four, is vital towards improving our general emotions. Passion has led to the destruction of a lot of relationships and the chequered history of humanity.

Many philosophers, among them, Seneca and Marcus Aurelius talked about the negative impact of anger and taught us how we could go through life without giving in to anger.

As we saw in chapter one, emotions are complex, and when in their full swing, they can be overwhelming. Consider the situation where you became so overwhelmed by anger that you did something that you regretted. Or feeling so fearful that you ended up in an embarrassing situation, or almost lost your life to the object of your fear. Emotions can and often are overpowering. As we saw in the beginning, we can control them, and we should be able to easily influence how we react when we feel overwhelmed by fear or shame or guilt or anger. Emotions are stimuli that nature intended to be what drives us to action. We act to rid ourselves of the excitement, rather than let the emotion act on our behalf.

After looking through ways in which you can subdue how you react to your emotions from chapter two through to four, in this chapter, we tie it all together. How do you use what you have learned to become a better person and build better relationships? How do you become a more emotionally adjusted person who has regard for others?

Become Aware of Yourself

Do you ever take the time to consider how you come across to others? Do you ever make the connection between how people act around you and how you act around them?

When you eventually learn how to control your emotions, to progress from here, you will then need to know how your emotional reaction to things and issues affect how others look at you. You will then achieve this by taking the time to sit with yourself and learn about how you put yourself forth to the environment around you. Stoicism gives us three virtues in for life - wisdom, morality, courage, and moderation. The stoic philosophy is one of the best philosophies that you can use to build better self-awareness.

It is through observing our thoughts that we become able to make the connection between them and how we act and react to the outside world and how it then acts and reacts towards us. Our bodies release chemicals with each thought, and it is these chemicals that then determine how we respond. When we are scared, our body produces adrenaline and osteocalcin that then lets us flee or fight off the threat. When stressed, the body produces cortisol, which sends signals in us that we are stressed and should act appropriately. When we are angry, our brain produces neurotransmitters called catecholamines, which then is what lead to how we bust out in anger. All this often happens before the part of the brain responsible for judgment, the cortex, kicks into action. In succession, the body then produces adrenaline and noradrenaline, which then puts you in a state of arousal, making you now ready to come to blows.

The thing about anger is that it tends to last long, even after the object of our hatred has gone. This situation then means that you will then express this anger in minor irritations. You will direct the anger to people that are not responsible for making you angry, thus costing you relationships. No wonder the Stoics call on us to altogether avoid getting angry. It harms you a lot more and stops you from processing things a bit more clearly.

It is through self-awareness that you will be able to judge better how you come across to others. Do you believe in the virtues that you claim? If you do not find what you claim, then chances are, people will read this, and they will then avoid you. This cognitive dissonance can be damaging to your relationships. You say that you care about others but then despise it when someone in the street asks you for money. You claim to be moral but then have no sense of it when someone you are close to is on the wrong.

When you reflect within yourself, you will be able to know where your strengths lie, what your weaknesses are, what you do not embody and espouse. You will understand what triggers emotional reactions in you and how you will then work towards having to reduce the influence they have on you.

Self-reflection is one of the key ways to build emotional intelligence as what we put out into the world is a reflection of how we are within. With a more accurate perception of who you are, you wlll begin to know where you need to improve to become better, where you are doing well and building on it and what you do not tolerate and won't work with when you come across someone.

This self-perception and acknowledgment of who you are, allows you to connect between your actions to how other people relate to you, something that many people, unfortunately, seem to lack. Have you ever come across someone so insufferable, yet lacking self-awareness such that you wonder just how they manage to get along in this world? Instead, pointing outwards for every error and mistake. Such is the effect of a lack of self-awareness. You will only see how the world reacts to you and remain blind to how you act out to the world. You will be unable to identify areas that you need to improve, which means that you will not build on yourself. Of course, when you are always blaming the other person, the relationship will not last.

Self-reflection improves how you present yourself to other people, and they will then respond positively, leading to better relationships. So, take time, each day to look at yourself.

Practice Self-Management

After self-awareness, comes self-management.

Self-management is the ability to direct yourself in a specific direction while being mindful and aware of your actions.

Let's try to think back at the time when you made a rational, favorable decision when you were under the temporary madness that emotions put us. Can you honestly remember? How many times did you then do this once you become aware of it?

As we have seen above, the chemical reaction in the brain when we become emotionally charged usually happens so fast before the part of our brain responsible for judgment kicks in. This reason is why you will come across instances of people making irrational, and sometimes stupid mistakes when they are highly emotively charged. It is for this reason that young couples in the throes of passion elope, or marry in haste. It is for our inability to be rational that we have fought wars that we could have avoided if we had taken just a little more time to think through before acting. It is possibly this reason that has led to people losing their jobs and broken relationships.

But, once you begin to practice self-awareness, this second part becomes rather easy to follow through. If anything, it is directly tied to self-awareness. Once you become aware of what triggers you, you will then become better at assessing situations and make preemptive measures on how you will act when the other person or the event push you to the edge.

When you choose to be emotionally present, you will then become able to take in devastating news or be in a stressful situation without it having to compromise your rational.

So, if you are someone who struggled with anger, this would mean that by becoming self-aware, you will then identify what triggers rage in you. Then, self-management follows through. Since you will be aware of what makes you angry, you will begin to make decisions that will help you fight the anger before it has taken complete control of you.

If you are extremely fearful, you will learn why you are nervous and then, make more deliberate actions towards overcoming that fear.

But to push through with this stage, you will need commitment and to put a lot of deliberate thought into it. Because we tend to want to stay the same, our brains will often talk us out of a movement for change. Yes, your mind is stopping you from pursuing your path to greater things.

Change is scary. For this reason, you will find that you will want to stay in familiar territory. Becoming deliberate in how you move and navigate around the world can be overwhelming. It will mean that you then get uncomfortable with the things you once enjoyed. It means coming to terms with your failings, becoming aware of how your actions, which you may have been doing without thought, affect your relationships and your overall mental health. So, it will not be easy to make the step towards managing how you react to your emotions. Plus, there is always that feeling of great satisfaction that comes with acting out your feelings. You feel you are justified in your actions. The adrenaline at that moment makes it seem like what you are doing is heroic. You are bold and courageous and not just emotional and irrational. So, it can then become addictive to want to keep yourself in this cycle of emotional turmoil. But while it may be for a moment, in the long-term, the effects of an emotional reaction to any situation is lasting.

When you become in touch with your emotions, you will then be able also to be more forgiving to other people that are struggling with their issues and will want to help them. As you become more forgiving of yourself, so do you become of others? When you are not in tune with your emotions, you will reflect that state other people. You become angry at another person with a short temper because you are also short-tempered. You mock another fearful person because you struggle with dread. All these issues work to make you unrelatable and unsociable.

When you manage your emotions better, it improves how you relate to people. Rather than reduce them to their emotional state of being, you see their struggle, because it is something that you have also struggled with/are struggling with and thus, can relate. You then exude charisma because you understand how the other person feels and help them begin the first steps towards managing their emotions better.

Improve Your Conflict Resolution Skills

We all want to be able to manage a situation without any adverse outcome, or at least, with minimal negative consequences. But how many of us really can do that? How many times have you intervened at a situation and arrived at an amicable conclusion?

Conflicts trigger strong emotions in us, which, when we do not resolve correctly, results in hurt and disappointment, and this could lead to breaking relationships.

Conflicts are often a sign of healthy relationships. When you can share your view with another person even when they do not agree with you, it shows that the relationship is open and the parties are open with each other. However, it is during conflicts that a lot of negative emotions arise. In battle, you become stressed, angry, fearful. Because of the high-voltage emotions, the chances of acting irrationally and in a way that damages the relationship are high. How, then, do you manage this delicate situation? How do you and the other party/parties get through this situation by maintaining the core of the relationship yet without being dishonest with each other just for civility?

So, how do you improve your conflict resolution skills?

Understand the conflict
During the conflict, it goes beyond just a disagreement. A battle stresses the body to see to it that there is a threat, even when there is none. So, to understand the conflict, be able to realize that the other person, just like you, is fearful and therefore, know that they do not have an issue with you.

So, take the time to know what caused the conflict? Were you on the wrong? If so, make a sincere apology? If your partner was on the wrong, you could bring them round in a respectful, non-condescending manner to their fault.

Throughout this process, it is essential to keep in mind that your problem is not with the other person, but rather, with an issue. So, avoid making remarks about the other person and instead, always ensure that you are speaking on the subject. So, rather than say "you are always hurting me', say instead "whatever you say always hurts me.' the second part brings attention to the person's utterances, rather than accuse them as a whole as is the first statement.

Understand the Needs of The Other Person

A second part of resolving a conflict is always to keep the other person in mind. With each back and forth, try to see their point of view. We all deserve to be respected and have our opinions considered. Therefore, to manage conflict better, always keep in mind the humanity of the other person. The understanding of other people is our role to humankind - to acknowledge the other person and their feelings, their needs, and their views. To see where they are coming from and why they see the world as they do, even when we do not agree with it.

Be Willing to Compromise

We all get the feeling of wanting to be right in a conflict. Thus, when the other person says something, you counter them with your hot-take, the result then being that throughout the battle, none of you listens to the other. This emotive back and forth will most often result in resentment and will lead to further breakdown in communication.

To manage conflict better, is necessary that you listen to the other person, and they then listen to you, and the two of you come to a compromise that will take into account the views of the other person.

Compromising doesn't mean that you waver on your principles. Instead, it shows that you value the relationship and the needs of the other person.

However, also note when you become the only one compromising, or the one making the most significant compromises after a conflict. This one-sided compromise is a symptom of a toxic relationship. While it is challenging to split settlement down the middle in a way that satisfies both parties, you can make it better by making sure that none of you holds the heavy side of things during every conflict.

When you make winning an argument or being right a priority, you will then not be willing to listen to the other person, and this will break down the communication further.

Focus on the Conflict In Front of You

It is often tempting to throw in previous encounters into a new conflict. You and the other person are arguing about whether or not to buy a new item, and then suddenly, you get a boost. "Remember that time you didn't (insert unrelated issue here)' you say. Suddenly, it devolves into the two of you just going on and on about an issue that wasn't part of the day's argument.

When we hold on to what was past, we become less able to make rational decisions. Rather than look to resolve the present conflict, we begin to dig deep into the past, trying to dig up something that will help you to win the argument or shut the other person up.

Be Willing to Let Go

Letting go can be a very delicate thing to do since you will often be conflicted as to whether you are making go or if you are sweeping the issue under the carpet.

But it is important to note that you should make a point of resolving the issue before you consider letting it go. You need to get to a situation where you can confidently answer "no' if you ask yourself if the problem still bothers you.

When you sweep things under the carpet, you will often still be bothered by them and would just be postponing them. So, to decide to let go, do so at a time when you are less angry or stressed and volatile. That will allow you to weigh the outcome of your decision rationally. If you still find yourself unable to let go, then you may not have resolved the issue.

Pick Your Battles

Not every potential conflict will need your input. When you become more in touch with your emotions, you will be able to know what is worth your effort and what is not.

Conflicts are high-stress situations and will drain you of your strength. So it is key to then, engage in only those conflicts that will result in an improvement of your perspective, well-being, and better understanding.

A lot of the time, most of the conflict we may find ourselves getting into will not be worth it. In economics, there is a principle called the Pareto Principle. We took this principle from Italian economist Vilfredo Pareto and it stated how he found that most of the land in Italy was under the control of a small percentage of the population (80% of land to 20% of the population). From this, came the belief that 20% of our actions shape 80% of the consequences. Using this rule, you will then realize that you should focus your efforts on conflicts and relationships that give you the best state of mind, the best instances for growth.

This rule will give you a peaceful state of mind as it will force you to sit down and try to identify what gives you great satisfaction as such, what requires your attention.

Relationship/Social Awareness

How do you tell if someone is saying what they mean when they aren't straightforward? How do you pry someone open when they aren't willing to be opened up?

In order to become emotionally intelligent and grow from the situations that you have faced, it is essential that you then channel your understanding of your emotional state also to understand the emotional being of the other person.

Social awareness is what allows us to develop relationships and maintain them.

When you make it a priority to understand the other person beyond the words that they speak, you will be able to gain a better understanding of them. So, how then, do you build social awareness?

Listen Keenly

Listening is one of those skills that, while important, is one that has hardly mastered. It is tough to listen, especially when you also have issues of your own going on. To relate well, or better with others, you must listen.

Listening allows you to hear, and the process then understands where the other person is coming from, how they see the world. Actively listening, which means repeating to the person what they say after they have said it, allows you to build a connection with the other person.

When you listen, you can put yourself in the other person's shoes, thus, understanding them better.

Be Aware of Non-verbal Cues

Psychologists say that we say a lot without speaking than we do speaking. But let us not dwell too much on whether this is true or not and instead, put ourselves in the situation where we do not feel comfortable expressing ourselves verbally. What do you often do?

If you are waiting for someone at a place where there are many other people, you may find yourself tapping impatiently at something, perhaps a table or the armrest of your chair. Or you may begin fiddling with something in your hands when you become anxious and restless.

We often send out these signals without our knowledge sometimes. Therefore, even when we say something that is in dissonance with our emotional state, our body language may betray us.

Thus, to build on your social awareness, be keen on what people are not saying. Look at how they carry themselves when they aren't speaking. Look at how they act when they cannot talk. Learning how to read these signals will help you become better at tailoring your message to match their state of being at the moment. So, you will try to make the anxious person relax by, say, cracking a joke before you proceed with your point.

When you show high awareness of people's actions during interactions, you will come across as someone who value them and what they say. This awareness will help you build a rapport faster with them. However, it is essential to note that you should do this expertly as you will come off as creepy if you are not careful. The key is to notice their non-verbal cues and interact with them in ways that make them feel the opposite of their reaction, all without making them feel watched.

Be Empathetic

To have empathy is the most significant way to build rapport. As we have seen earlier in chapter five, to develop your compassion, you need to be aware of who you are first.

But, empathy is a problematic state of being to master. Because of our belief in the superiority of our being and ideas, to be empathetic will mean that you look at other people with an acknowledgment of their humanity. Empathy means that you will try to put yourself in their shoes and interact with them from their perspective. It is easier said than done, though.

How many instances have you found yourself unable to understand why a person will believe the things that they do? How many times have you made final judgments about someone without giving yourself a chance to glimpse from where they are coming?

We often make this oversight a lot of the times, which then shows that empathy is something that we should practice.

To be empathetic is to acknowledge the humanity of the other person, even when we do not agree with them. It means that you know that the person that was rude to you may have been under their stresses. It means that you understand why someone else made a drastic decision that seemed illogical and stupid.

Allowing others the room to be human and to err is a significant strand of emotional growth and intelligence. It means then that in your interactions with people, you will listen to them more, you will agree with them more and contradict them without belittling them. To be empathetic will make you cherish your friendships and play your part because you understand our human need of wanting love and recognition, called the law of esteem.

So, practice empathy when you interact with others. To begin this, whenever you are talking to someone, and they say something that you do not agree with, rather than interrupt them with your beliefs, as them why they view the world as they do. Once you learn about them, you can then use persuasion to try and give them a different perspective.

This practice, of course, will be hard in situations where the issue of contention is highly emotive and divisive. And it becomes even harder to empathize with the other person when they appear hell-bent on remaining to their ways.

Well, it is here that you apply the earlier lesson in conflict management - know when to walk away/cut your losses. You cannot empathize someone out of their ignorance that they want to maintain. If they are willing to have a sobering discussion about it, then beautiful. However, if they seem to not listen to you as much as you listen to them, walk away, because emotional intelligence is also about knowing when to walk away.

Channel Emotions Productively

To bring your emotions under control is not to mean that you cannot feel these emotions. It is also not that you cannot find ways to express them.

Mark Manson, of the *Subtle Art of Not Giving a Fuck* fame, stated that you could not control yourself from feeling, but how you react to how you think is what is essential.

Intense emotions have a way of rewiring our brains. They are disruptive and cause us disequilibrium. Since we are learning how to become more emotionally intelligent, I will not mention destructive, but we have seen how they can be catastrophic, even more, positive feelings like joy or happiness. When emotions within us begin to run, significant, the chemical reactions in the body lead to various changes in us, which then means that we become more focused, the focal point of our attention being the person or event that is causing us the joy or happiness or distress and anger.

And to be emotional is then to be ripe for various surges of human feats. When we look at the annals of our history, we often get to see how people turned their emotions into art or literature or social movement. Think of how people who suffered great grief and a sense of loss used to make social movements. We can look at how mothers who suffered significant injury make movements that address the issue that led to their loss, e.g., Mothers Against Drunken Driving.

When we look at anger, we see it as a negative emotion. And it is true. Anger is a passion which we can live better with when we have it under our control. We can also see how we can use passion to do good.

Human rights movements and many movements for social change often have people who are fed up with the situation as they are and so, use the frustration to make their voices heard.

When you begin to make yourself more self-aware, you will realize that through every emotional upheaval that you experience, there are ways in which you can channel it positively. Your grief could make you more willing to address the situation that led to your loss. Your joy could make you want to discuss what made you miserable so that you do not experience it again. Anger can drive you to become more focused and drive social change. All these help you become a more valuable member of society, even when you do not get recognition or applause for it. You do it to improve your surroundings.

This act of channeling our emotions to constructive activity is known as positive psychology, which calls us to not only embrace our positive emotions but also come to terms with our negative ones and embrace them too. They exist for a reason, the reason being that, more than positive emotions, negative emotions are great catalysts for change.

So, how do you begin to channel the emotions more constructively?

Think if It's Worth Exploring

When we say that you can use your emotions to drive change and make a positive impact, be in the know that it may not always be the case and that sometimes, your desire to channel your emotions could not be compelling because whatever makes you angry could be something beyond your control.

So, in this case, take a moment to think of expressing the emotions is necessary. At times, you are better off taking time out to let the emotions cool down as you avoid high-octane situations that could trigger you.

Monitor and Correct

To be able to channel your emotions positively means to be in constant touch with what triggers you, how you react to it, and how it affects your moods and actions. Then, map out the adverse reactions you take when in your emotional trance. Then, create ways to make it work for you, and as well as for others.

When angry, for example, you can use the razor-sharp focus of the rage to work on your projects or to begin your workout routine. When in grief, you can use the muse that that clouds us during pain to create art or literature to express it.

Always make a point of monitoring your reactions. Every. Time. This monitoring is hard, as it will need you to be always alert, but if you want to become a better person, a more social person, you will need to be aware of your emotional reactions.

Know Your Limits

Embracing your emotions should also come with the knowledge that you have your limits. Become aware of whether you are becoming addicted to getting a high out of your feelings. Remember, the key is not to make the emotions your muse for expression but rather, using your inspiration to channel your creativity when you are emotional.

This call then means that you should be aware of how you act when you have calmed down. Create a situation where you give yourself a short time within which you hold onto emotion and channel it. After which, be willing to let go. Scientists have noted that anger especially, tends to remain active in the body for hours or even days after the initial trigger of your anger has passed. This revelation then means that you become susceptible to triggering at the slightest inconveniences. The reaction can then destroy relationships and make you unwilling to compromise with others. So, become aware of your limits and know when just to let go. This awareness will improve your well-being generally, as well as make you better in your relationship with others.

Boost Your Performance

We all experience self-doubt in different scenarios. Even when we are confident in our skills, there will still be situations where you find yourself lacking confidence in your abilities. Self-doubt can be crippling. But just like any other emotion, you can use it to make yourself become a higher performer.

So, when you experience self-doubt, make a point of seeking out someone more experienced in your field and learn from them. Alternatively, since self-doubt makes you doubt your abilities or skills, you can leverage it as a motivation to keep doing it in a bid to improve yourself. When you do it, you become better at what you. In time, you find that you are in a level of mastery of your skills or abilities.

You can do this with regret too. If you made a wrong choice, you could use the guilt that comes with it to push yourself forward. You create a situation in your head where you do not want to go back to feeling regret, so you use it to propel yourself forward. Who will stop you?

When you learn to channel emotions more positively, you will quickly realize that you will not need to have an external motivator to propel yourself. The surges of emotions will be enough to give you the propulsion you need.

Share Your Knowledge

When we get into relationships, whether friendships or romances, we always want to feel part of the other person. Through an exchange of ideas and experiences, we make each other comfortable and vulnerable, creating a bond that we trust will be productive to us in the end.

When you have gone through all the steps to become a better person, it is vital that you then make a point of making those around you become aware of their failings and learn from you.

Sharing is one of the profound ways in which we show that we are vulnerable with each other. It is the result of you being able to relate to the other person. For many reasons, and to many of us, sharing is often something that we either are unwilling to do or uncomfortable doing.

This reaction is often born from our insecurity, one of the biggest causes of failure in relationships. Because of the fear of being upstaged, people will avoid sharing knowledge, skills with others. This situation, of course, causes friction and will result in a breakdown of communication in the relationship and eventually a break-up.

When you become a more emotionally intelligent person, you become comfortable in the knowledge that you are not perfect, and that's okay. You know that the other person is better than you in some instances and areas and that is okay. What you are focused on is self-improvement, and your understanding of our emotional needs means that you will be willing to share your improvement tips with the others, as you know that, even at their best, your friends or partner(s) remain human as so, still have a crippling doubt of themselves.

When you share, you communicate that you care. Our relationships flourish when we show the other people that love us that we are on the lookout for them. In turn, they also develop the same towards us.

However, this may not be the case sometimes. There are many cases where one party was more generous and giving, and the other party just took it all for granted. Still giving is often a sign of the other person being a narcissist or at the very least, a self-absorbed asshole. They consider the fact that someone committed to them is a sign of their charm and superiority. To them, the other person and their needs are worthless. What is important is what they want. This selfishness, of course, creates a delicate balance. But, as someone who is developing your emotional intelligence, you will be able to pick this out before you establish a secure connection with the person.

Keep Secrets

One of how we build connections, according to psychologists, is often through gossip. Many researchers have concluded that we usually bond better when we find common ground about another person which allows us to then create a rapport with the other person as it gives us something mutual that we often need when we want to create a connection.

However, this revelation has meant that many people, especially those that lack emotional intelligence, become more willing to share their secrets and those of their loved ones with any charming stranger.

One of the ways that we can build and maintain relationships is through respect of the other person's confidentiality. This result is because when you respect the other person and are emotionally astute, you will want to maintain their trust. It is trust that develops from all the others. When you are empathetic, you become more understanding of the other person, and thus, gain their confidence. When you are honest, you communicate that you are trustworthy. When you make a point of helping others become better people, you tell them that they can put their belief in you. It all builds up to trust as you can see. It is trust when the other person becomes vulnerable to you and shares their deepest secrets.

So, as you get more in touch with your emotions and who you are, then you will be in a position to want to maintain the relationships, you value the bond and thus, will do the right things to sustain them, which includes confidentiality.

When you find yourself eager to share your friends' secrets just because the person you have met sounds and looks decent, you may not be emotionally mature. Take a moment and pause. Why do you want to share your friends' secrets with this stranger? Do you value them if you do?

Gaining trust and maintaining it is hard. To do that requires that you are a person who has a high EQ (emotional quotient). You understand that the other person is sharing with you, not because they are stupid, but because they feel like they have an ear in you. Don't break it. Always make a point of maintaining and keeping your end of the agreement.

But, what if the other person is the one that breaks my trust? You ask.

It is true that not every person that we meet will turn out to be a great friend. Because of our bias on first impressions, many people with sinister intentions will often be charming and accommodating at first. The charm is so that they can gain our trust. If you find yourself having to deal with the other person breaking your confidence, the best thing to do is to acknowledge what you are going through. You will be angry and confused and at a loss. Acknowledge these feelings, then practice what you have learned to help you cope.

Conclusion

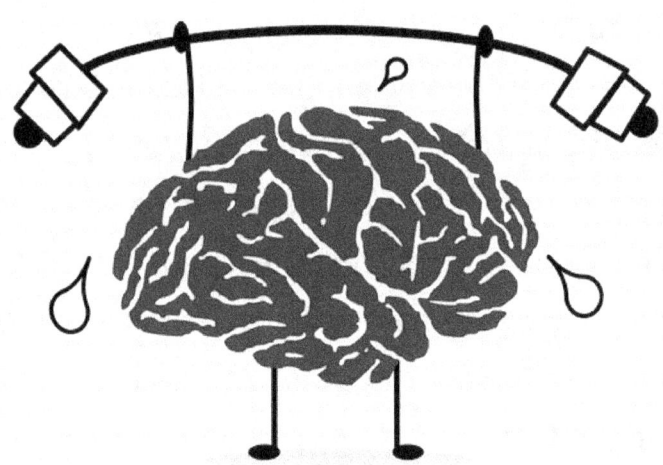

Emotions are necessary, and they are with us in everything that we do. In every decision that we make, there is an emotion connected to it. Thus, mastering it is the
key.

In this book, we have learned:
- What emotions are and how they work. This understanding has allowed us to delve deeper into the essence of emotions into our being.

- We have looked at how emotions, when they become active, can be destructive and thus, looked at how emotional intelligence can help us cope.
- We have also looked into how we can manage stress, fears, and crippling negative thoughts. Emotions have a way of shaping how we view the world; thus, keeping track to them to keep them in check is vital.
- You have also learned how to manage our anger and how to make the best of our emotions to build our relationships. After all, emotions help us build relationships and are also critical in how we destroy them. Thus, looking at how we can develop better relationships around our emotions is worth learning.

www.ingramcontent.com/pod-product-compliance
Lightning Source LLC
Chambersburg PA
CBHW071627080526
44588CB00010B/1305